LUSH & LIVELY
FLOWERS YOU CAN PAINT

SHARON HAMILTON, MDA

NORTH LIGHT BOOKS
CINCINNATI, OHIO
www.artistsnetwork.com

ABOUT THE AUTHOR

Sharon began her career with a degree in commercial photography from the Art Institute of Pittsburgh. She worked and taught in the photographic field for a number of years. Using the disciplines of seeing and understanding light from her photographic work, she refined that knowledge into her own unique style of realistic decorative painting.

Sharon became a Certified Decorative Artist in the Society of Decorative Painters in 1990. She successfully completed her Master levels in Floral, Still Life and Strokework to earn her Master Decorative Artist designation in 2001.

Sharon has been published in *PaintWorks*, *CraftWorks*, *The Decorative Painter*, Nihon Vogue *Paint Craft* and JDPA's *Decorative Painting*. She had the honor of having her work selected for exhibition at the Nihon Vogue Decorative Painting Gallery of the World in Tokyo, Japan in 2001. In addition, Sharon has authored six books on painting floral and still life subjects using her acrylic with oil glazing technique.

Sharon has taught at thirteen national conventions held by the Society of Decorative Painters. She teaches weekly classes in her local area and travel teaches throughout the U.S. and Canada. She resides in southeastern Pennsylvania with her husband and two daughters.

Lush & Lively Flower Painting for Decorative Artists. Copyright © 2004 by Sharon Hamilton. Manufactured in China. All rights reserved. The patterns and drawings in this book are for the personal use of the decorative painter. By permission of the author and publisher, they may be either hand-traced or photocopied to make single copies, but under no circumstances may they be resold or republished. No part of the text, patterns, paintings or instructions, whether in whole or in part, may be used for profit or reproduced in any form, except as noted above, without the express written permission of the copyright holder. No other part of this book may be reproduced in any form or by any electronic or mechanical means including information storage and retrieval systems without permission in writing from the publisher, except by a reviewer, who may quote brief passages in a review. The content of this book has been thorougly reviewed for accuracy. However, the author and publisher disclaim any liability for any damages, losses or injuries that may result from the use or misuse of any product or information presented herein. It is the purchaser's responsibility to read and follow all instructions and warnings on all product labels. Published by North Light Books, an imprint of F&W Publications, Inc., 4700 East Galbraith Road, Cincinnati, Ohio 45236. (800) 289-0963 First edition.

08 07 06 05 04   5 4 3 2 1

Library of Congress Cataloging-in-Publication Data

Hamilton, Sharon
    Lush & lively flowers you can paint / by Sharon Hamilton.
      p. cm.
    Includes index.
    ISBN 1-58180-443-1 (pbk. : alk. paper)
    1. Painting--Technique. 2. Decoration and ornament--Plant forms. 3. Flowers in art. I. Title: Lush and lively flowers you can paint. II. Title.

TT385.H343 2004
745.7'23--dc22   2003061416

Edited by Maureen Mahany Berger
Designed by Joanna Detz
Production coordinated by Kristen Heller
Photographed by Tim Grondin and Christine Polomsky

METRIC CONVERSION CHART

To convert	to	multiply by
Inches	Centimeters	2.54
Centimeters	Inches	0.4
Feet	Centimeters	30.5
Centimeters	Feet	0.03
Yards	Meters	0.9
Meters	Yards	1.1
Sq. Inches	Sq. Centimeters	6.45
Sq. Centimeters	Sq. Inches	0.16
Sq. Feet	Sq. Meters	0.09
Sq. Meters	Sq. Feet	10.8
Sq. Yards	Sq. Meters	0.8
Sq. Meters	Sq. Yards	1.2
Pounds	Kilograms	0.45
Kilograms	Pounds	2.2
Ounces	Grams	28.3
Grams	Ounces	0.035

ACKNOWLEDGMENTS

Let me first thank my family for all the things they've had to endure while I've been busy painting, writing or not at home. You have been so supportive, thank you.

Thank you, Gretchen Cagle, for believing in me and championing my start in the decorative painting field.

To all my students who are never afraid to dive in feet first—your enthusiasm is catching and keeps me going. You have touched my life and I hope I have touched yours in a way that you can carry with you through your lifetime. I love you!

Thank you to all the suppliers for this book who have been so wonderful and generous: DecoArt Americana, ColArt America, Loew-Cornell, Magic Metallics, Painters Paradise, Gretchen Cagle Publications, Barb Watson's Brushworks, Wood-Ware and Wood Concepts. Your continued support frees me to create and inspire!

And thank you to all of you at North Light: Maureen Berger, my editor; Kathy Kipp, for believing in my work and pushing for this book, and Tim Grondin, my photographer.

Dedication

This book is dedicated to my family, my husband, Chuck, and our daughters, Elizabeth and Chelsea. Without your unending patience and love this book would not have been possible. You have filled my life with joy and so much love that I am inspired to put these feelings into my paintings. I am so thankful for all of your support, and for lifting my spirits during the times that I wasn't so sure of myself.

To my dad, who has inspired me throughout my lifetime with his love of nature and his ability to grow wonderful plants and trees from this beautiful earth. His nurturing of everything green has had a profound effect upon the way in which I see flowers and nature. I have learned so much about life from him. Thanks, Dad. I love you.

TABLE OF CONTENTS

Introduction 6

CHAPTER 1
Supplies 8

CHAPTER 2
Techniques 10

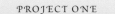

PROJECT ONE

Wildflower Clock
page 18

PROJECT TWO

Tin Heart Ornaments
page 30

PROJECT THREE

Daylilies Spice Bin
page 44

PROJECT FOUR

Yellow Tulips Mail Keeper
page 54

PROJECT FIVE

Wisteria Tray
page 64

PROJECT SIX

Dogwood Box

page 74

PROJECT SEVEN

Sunflower Tray

page 86

PROJECT EIGHT

Fuchsia Heart Box

page 98

PROJECT NINE

Morning Glory Birdhouse

page 108

PROJECT TEN

Daffodil & Butterfly Box

page 118

Resources 126

Index 127

INTRODUCTION

I live in constant wonder of nature's beauty in the world that surrounds me. Through painting flowers and bugs, I try to bring the beauty I see every day to you. I have tried to capture the excitement and joy that the natural world brings to me, and it is my hope that my artwork will touch your life as nature has touched mine.

My work has been inspired by the many gardens that I have planted and photographed over the years. Each season brings excitement as I watch the blossoms unfold. The way the warm afternoon sun touches delicately across a petal or the way a dewdrop drips from a leaf can spark a new vision. This vision is something that I want to share with you. All things are better when shared with others.

By working through each design step by step you will be able to recreate these emotions that I have tried to convey to you. With practice, the techniques that I have presented will make you a more skilled painter. Please don't allow yourself to become discouraged if your end result is different than mine. Expressing yourself creatively makes each painting your own. Each painter has her own personality and it does come out in your painting—so express yourself!

It is my sincere hope that you enjoy painting each of the designs in this book and that you learn to love nature as I do.

From my heart to yours...

Sharon Hamilton, MDA

SUPPLIES

Brushes

Good quality brushes are an essential key to brush control. A brush with a sharp chisel edge will respond well to all the floating techniques that you will be learning. A worn-out scruffy brush will yield only headaches and not give you the final result that you desire.

I've chosen mainly Loew-Cornell brushes. They are a superior quality brush that will hold up well. The Comfort brushes that are used for the acrylic portion of the painting are shaped to allow your fingers to fall into the proper placement and reduce hand fatigue. The Arttec sable brushes, used for the oil glazing, have the perfect "spring" to the hair that I find desirable when working with oil paints.

Loew-Cornell Brushes
- Comfort Filbert Series 3500
- Comfort Shader Series 3300
- Maxine's Oval Mop Series 270
- Arttec Red Sable Flat Series 124
- Arttec Red Sable Filbert Series 128
- Comfort Mid-Length Liner Series 3370
- Jackie Shaw Mid-Length Liner Series J-S 10/0

Raphaël Brushes
- Pure Kolinsky Red Sable Series 8404 no. 1 round

Basic Supplies

The photo on the facing page shows many of the basic supplies I used to paint the projects in this book. Most if not all can be found in art and craft supply stores. Each project lists the specific materials and paint colors you will need to complete that project, but here is an overall list of the basic painting supplies I use.

- Loew-Cornell Brush Tub II
- Waxed palette pad for palette blending
- Wingate Artist Palette. Reusable acrylic palette.
- Scott Shop Towels. Use these for a wet palette.
- Tracing paper
- Double ball-tipped stylus. Use for transferring the pattern.
- White and gray graphite paper
- Fine-grit sandpaper
- DecoArt Americana Acrylics
- DecoArt Dazzling Metallics
- DecoArt Gel Stains
- DecoArt Staining/Antiquing Medium
- DecoArt Faux Glazing Medium
- DecoArt Multi-Purpose Sealer. I prefer this because I can mix my base color with it equally and then base and seal the project in one step.
- Magic Metallic Matte Interior Sealer
- Magic Metallic: Gold, Copper and Dark Bronze
- Magic Metallic Patinas: Green and Aqua Blue
- Winsor & Newton Blending & Glazing Medium
- Winsor & Newton Artists' Oil Colours
- Winsor & Newton ArtGel. Use as a final soap for all of your brushes.
- Krylon Matte Finish #1311
- Krylon Satin Finish #7002
- Krylon Leafing Pen: 18Kt. Gold and Silver. This is an easy way to achieve a gold or silver leafing effect.
- Betterway Brush Cleaning Fluid and Oil Paint Solvent
- Loew-Cornell Cleaning Jar
- Loew-Cornell Painting Knife
- Jo Sonja's Crackle Medium. This gives a fine crackling effect.
- Jo Sonja's Magic Mix. This allows the paint to have a longer open time.

CHAPTER TWO

TECHNIQUES

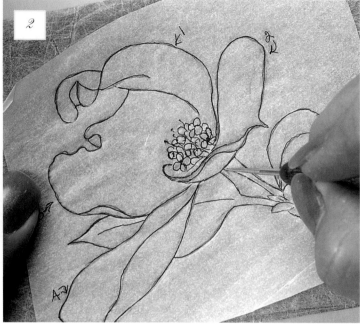

1 TRACING THE PATTERN

Tape a piece of tracing paper over the pattern. Use a fine-line marker to trace the lines of the pattern carefully. Remember, if your tracing has misshapen lines then your completed painting will definitely be misshapen.

2 TRANSFERRING THE PATTERN

Tape the tracing onto your prepared surface. Place a piece of white or gray graphite paper under the tracing. Use a stylus to transfer the main lines of the pattern. I try to use as little pressure as possible when pressing on the stylus; I use only enough pressure to vaguely see the transferred lines. It is very important to follow the lines on your tracing to avoid a problem with misshapen elements.

When using gray graphite paper, use an old piece if transferring onto a light background color.

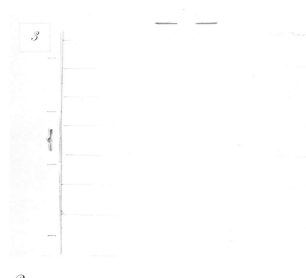

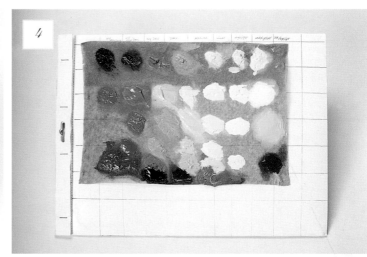

3 LABELING AN ACRYLIC PALETTE

When you begin to set up your acrylic palette, try to keep it as organized as possible. Use a fine–line waterproof marker to label the values across the top of a waxed or Wingate palette. Begin with the lightest value at the top right and work through all of the values, ending with the darkest one at the left. Next, label the elements to be painted along the left side of the palette in the order that they will be painted: i.e. Background, Leaves, Petals, etc. Keeping the palette organized makes it very easy to pick up exactly the value that is indicated in the project.

4 SETTING UP AN ACRYLIC PALETTE

Take a sheet of blue shop towel and place it in the brush basin filled with water. Pull out the paper towel and squeeze a little bit of the water out of it. Don't squeeze too much out; it still should be very wet. The wet paper towel acts as a wick to keep the paint moist during the painting session for easier floating. Lay the paper towel down on the labeled palette and smooth it out. The palette is now ready for the paint mixes to be placed on it. Please don't substitute another type of paper towel as they are not strong enough.

5 FULLY LOADING YOUR ACRYLIC BRUSH

Use a damp brush that has been blotted on paper toweling. Place the tips of the brush into the edge of the paint and pull outward onto the palette paper. Hold the brush at an angle while pulling and loading it.

Keep a spray bottle full of water handy to mist the paint and paper towel frequently during the painting session. Paint that forms a skin and becomes sticky is nearly impossible to float! I have also found it helpful to cover my palette with plastic wrap if I have to stop painting for a while. Simply spray the paints with water and then cover them with the plastic wrap. The palette can be kept workable for a very long time by doing this.

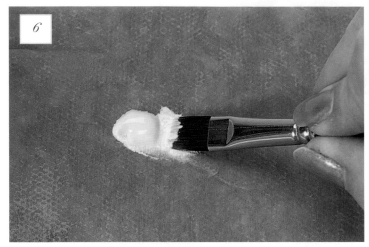

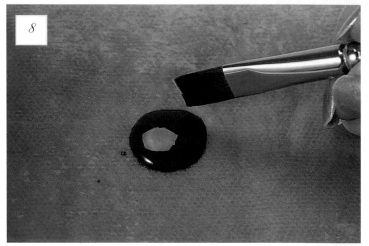

6 Load the paint close to but not into the ferrule of the brush. Flip the brush over and repeat the process. Work the paint into the brush hairs by repeating this process until the brush is fully loaded.

7 ACRYLIC BASECOATING

Fully load the brush and then place it onto the edge of the element being basecoated. If necessary, use the chisel edge of the brush to begin and add pressure as the stroke is pulled. Broaden the stroke, following the contour of the element. Repeat this process until the element is fully based.

8 SIDELOADING YOUR ACRYLIC BRUSH

Use a damp brush that has been blotted on paper toweling. Dip the corner of the brush into the paint.

9 Lay the brush flat on the surface of the waxed palette paper and pull short, downward strokes to load the paint across the width of the brush. This action creates a puddle of wet paint.

10 Flip the brush over and place the loaded side of the brush into the wet paint puddle and pull more short, downward strokes. Loading the brush this way allows for a heavier amount of paint to be deposited in one corner while the paint fades off across the edge of the brush.

11 FLOAT

Sideload the brush and begin the float on the chisel edge, gradually adding pressure as the brush is pulled. Pull the brush, lift and then pull it again. Repeat this process to make the float. Let up on the pressure and taper the end of the float using the chisel edge of the brush.

12 WALKED FLOAT

Sideload the brush and hold it at a 90–degree angle to the surface. Work the chisel edge of the brush in an up–and–down motion, following the contour of the petal or leaf. The chisel edge of the brush creates a veinlike or rippled appearance for a petal or leaf.

13 BACK-TO-BACK FLOAT

Sideload the brush and walk a float downward, then flip the brush over and float it against the solid edge of the previous float. This type of float is used to make a wide float through the middle of an element. For example, a back–to–back float would be used down the center of a leaf to create the shadow area for a vein, or to create a highlight through the center of a petal to make it appear to be bending.

14 BLENDING WITH A FILBERT USING THE FLAT EDGE

Use this type of blending to blend the soft edge of a regular float. Dip the filbert into water and then blot the excess on paper toweling. The brush should be damp to the touch. Hold the filbert at an angle and almost flat to the surface. Place the brush along the soft edge of the float and pull it outward slightly. Be careful not to disrupt the more solid portion of the float.

15 BLENDING WITH THE TIPS OF A FILBERT

Use this type of filbert blending with a walked or back-to-back float. Dip the filbert into water and blot the excess. The brush is damp to the touch. Hold the filbert at a 90–degree angle to the edge of the surface and use the tips of the brush to pull the lines outward and away from the float. Again, follow the contour of the leaf or petal.

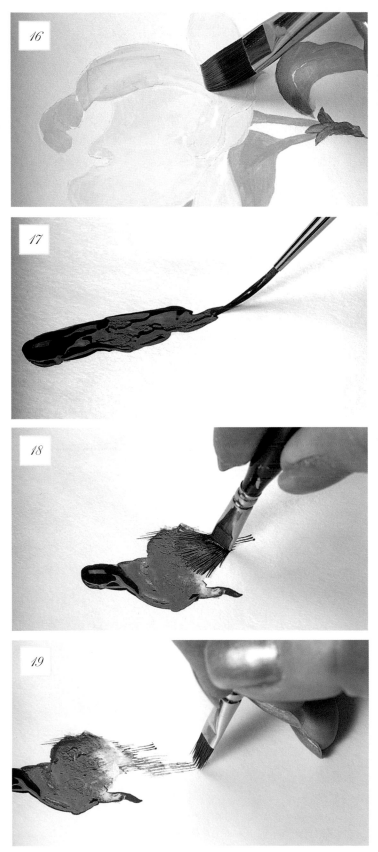

16 COLOR WASH

Dip the brush into water, blot it slightly and then dip the corner of the brush into the paint. Palette blend the color into the entire brush and then wash this thin layer of paint over the desired area.

17 LOADING A LINER

Dip the liner into water and then place the tip of the brush into the edge of the paint. Pull the brush while twisting it outward onto the waxed palette, loading the paint into the body of the brush. Allow the paint to almost reach the brush ferrule. Repeat the process until the hairs are fully loaded.

18 LOADING A RAKE

Dip the rake into water and then use the tips of the brush to pull some thinned paint from the base of the paint puddle. Load the paint into the hairs by pushing down on the brush and working the hairs back and forth into the thinned paint that was pulled out onto the palette.

19

Work the excess paint out of the paint hairs on the palette by standing the brush at a 90–degree angle and pull it lightly across the waxed palette. When you see fine lines being formed by the individual hairs of the brush, then it is ready to use on your painting.

I prefer to work with a filbert rake rather than a straight rake because the filbert doesn't leave harsh, straight lines when I begin to pull the stroke. The filbert is a much more natural way to create the fine lines needed for flowers or leaves.

20 CLEANING UP THE EDGES

Sometimes when making a float the brush can go outside the basecoated area by mistake, making the edges of the object messy. To clean up the edges, sideload a large shader brush with the background color and place the loaded edge of the brush on the background beside the misshapen edge. Pull a float along the edge of the mistake. Repeat the float if needed until the messy edge is no longer visible.

21 SETTING UP AN OIL PALETTE

Choose a palette that is impervious to oil paint so the oil is not leached from the pigment. Set up your oil palette in much the same order as the acrylic palette. Place all the tube colors across the top of the palette. You need only a small dab of oil paint squeezed out. Begin at the right and work to the left in this order: Titanium White, Cadmium Yellow Pale, Indian Yellow, Alizarin Crimson, Permanent Alizarin Crimson, Olive Green, Charcoal Grey and Payne's Grey.

22 MAKING WARM WHITE FOR OIL GLAZING

Most of the projects call for the use of Warm White and it must be mixed. Use about a dime–size (18mm diam.) dab of Titanium White and add a very tiny amount of Cadmium Yellow Pale to it. The photo shows the approximate ratio of yellow to white. The resulting color will be an off–white without being too yellow. In the photo the mix is shown underneath the Titanium White paint.

If you are building up the highlights on a leaf and the warm white mix appears too chalky, then make the mix a bit more to the yellow side by adding a little more yellow to the white.

23 MAKING THE YELLOW OIL GLAZE

In some projects, Yellow Glaze is used in place of the plain glazing medium. To make Yellow Glaze, pour some glazing medium onto the palette and then pick up a very small amount of Indian Yellow on the palette knife. The photo shows the ratio of paint to glazing medium.

24
Mix the Indian Yellow oil paint into the glazing medium for a slightly tinted glaze. Too much Indian Yellow will make the objects that are being glazed too yellow, so care must be taken to avoid adding too much paint to the glazing medium.

25 LOADING A BRUSH WITH OIL PAINT

Load only a very small amount of oil paint onto the sable brush. Use the corner of the brush to pull a small amount of paint from paint pile. Work the side of the brush into the paint that was pulled onto the palette until the brush has enough to apply to the painted surface.

WILDFLOWER CLOCK

Wildflowers are a favorite of mine because they come in so many different colors, shapes and sizes. These lovely flowers can be found growing wild along roadways and in meadows and woodlands. As I have walked through them I could smell their sweet fragrance floating in the breeze.

In this lesson you will be working with a variety of these wildflowers, from the airy Queen Anne's Lace to the very fine petals of fleabane. Each requires particular, detailed techniques to create its unique qualities.

I've incorporated several different techniques on the clock casing to lend it a country feeling. You will work with crackling on the background and then learn how to antique it with a darker value so the crackle is more apparent. I have used a combination of dark green paint overlaid with gold, and then treated with a green patina. Again, using colors that relate to the leaves helps pull the whole theme of the clock together.

This clock comes complete with four panels to paint. Take a walk and gather your own bunch of wildflowers. Then get your creative juices flowing and work up another design or two for your clock!

This pattern may be hand-traced or photo-copied for personal use only. Enlarge at 133% to bring it up to full size

COLORS & MATERIALS

Antique Green (DA)

Antique Teal (DA)

Avocado (DA)

Blue Chiffon (DA)

Celery Green (DA)

Charcoal Grey (DA)

Citron Green (DA)

Cool White (DA)

Dried Basil Green (DA)

Eggshell (DA)

Evergreen (DA)

Jade Green (DA)

Light Buttermilk (DA)

Light Parchment (DA)

Limeade (DA)

Milk Chocolate (DA)

Payne's Grey (DA)

Petal Pink (DA)

Pink Chiffon (DA)

Primary Yellow (DA)

Rookwood Red (DA)

Soft Lilac (DA)

Soft Sage (DA)

Vivid Violet (DA)

Warm White (DA)

Country Blue (DA)

Cadmium Yellow Pale (WN)

Charcoal Grey (WN)

Indian Yellow (WN)

Olive Green (WN)

Purple Madder Alizarin (WN)

Titanium White (WN)

Warm White mix (WN) (*See* page 16)

Payne's Grey (WN)

SURFACE

Domed wooden clock case with removable front panel from Wood Concepts (*see* Resources)

PAINTS
DA = DecoArt Americana Acrylics
WN = Winsor & Newton Artists Oils

BRUSHES: LOEW-CORNELL

Comfort Series 3550 Glaze/ Wash 1/2-inch (12mm), 3/4-inch (19mm), 1-inch (25mm). Comfort Series 3600 Oval Wash 3/4-inch (19mm). La Corneille Series 7550 Wash/Glaze 1 1/2-inch (37mm). Maxine's Oval Mop 3/4-inch (19mm). Fabric Series FAB Round no. 3. Comfort Series 3300 Shader nos. 4, 6, 8, 10, 12. Comfort Series 3500 Filbert nos. 8, 10. Comfort Series 3370 Mid-Length Liner no. 10/0. Comfort Series 3000 Round no. 3. Comfort Series Filbert Rake 3520 1/4-inch (6mm). Arttec Red Sable Series 124 Flat no. 6. Arttec Red Sable Series 126 Filbert no. 6. Arttec Red Sable Series 130B Bright nos. 8, 10.

ADDITIONAL SUPPLIES

DecoArt Multi-Purpose Sealer & Transparent Gel Medium. Jo Sonja Crackle Medium. Winsor & Newton Blending & Glazing Medium. Magic Metallics: Gold Metallic, Green Patina. Interior Matte Sealer.

1 Remove the wooden panel from the clock and set it aside. Make a mix of Soft Sage + Light Buttermilk 1:2; then base the inside and outside surfaces of the clock casing with a 1-inch (25mm) wash brush. When the base color is dry, use a ¾-inch (19mm) oval brush to apply a layer of crackle medium. Apply it in one direction and do not rework any of the areas where it has been applied. Use a hair dryer or allow it to completely air dry.

2 Make a mix of Antique Teal + Charcoal Grey 1:1, then mix it with Transparent Gel Medium 1:3 for a dark green antiquing mix. Apply the antiquing to each side of the casing with a 1½-inch (37mm) wash brush and then wipe the excess with a lint-free paper towel. Work on one section at a time until the entire casing has been completed. Blend the antiquing from one section to another with a ¾-inch (19mm) mop.

3 Make a mix of Antique Teal + Charcoal Grey 1:1 and mix it with equal parts of sealer. Using this mix and a ½-inch (12mm) wash brush, basecoat the trim on the clock casing. When dry, apply a layer of Magic Metallic Gold Metallic over the green trim and allow it to dry. Use a ¾-inch (19mm) wash brush to apply Magic Metallic Green Patina to the gold areas. As the patina dries, it will oxidize and cause the green patina to appear. Complete the trim by drybrushing Gold Metallic onto it for a scuffed effect. Apply a coat of matte sealer to the trim area with a ½-inch (12mm) wash brush.

4 Use a 1-inch (25mm) wash brush and basecoat the front clock casing panel with Soft Sage. The background is a series of floats applied with a slip-slap method for a mottled appearance. Sideload Soft Sage + Milk Chocolate 6:1, onto a ¾-inch (19mm) wash brush and slip-slap it in the light open area in the upper center behind the Queen Anne's Lace. Sideload Soft Sage + Light Buttermilk 1:2, onto the flat and slip-slap it within the previous light area. Use a damp ½-inch (12mm) oval to blend. Float a tint of thinned Citron Green along the edges of the panel and then slip-slap it in the lower two-thirds section. Use the damp filbert to blend. Float a darker tint with thinned Dried Basil Green in the upper-right corner and the lower corners.

Sideload a ¾-inch (19mm) wash brush with Celery Green and float it in the upper corners. Reload and float it in the lower corners and slip-slap it in the lower third of the panel. Use a damp ½-inch (12mm) oval to blend. Sideload thinned Warm White mix + Rookwood Red 2:1 onto a ¾-inch (19mm) wash brush and float it in the upper-right corner and along the right edge of the panel. Sideload Avocado + Celery Green 1:1, float it across the base and slip-slap it in the lower third of the panel; use a damp filbert to blend. Deepen the corners and lower edge of the panel with a float of Evergreen + Charcoal Grey 2:1, and then a float of Antique Teal + Charcoal Grey 1:1, within the previous float. Transfer the main pattern lines when the panel has dried.

5 Basecoat the stems using a no. 10/0 liner loaded with thinned Queen Anne's Lace Leaves & Stems "Medium" mix, Antique Green + Citron Green + Celery Green 2:1:1. Load a no. 3 round brush with the Medium mix and base-coat the leaves. Use a ¼-inch (6mm) filbert rake loaded with thinned Medium mix to pull stems attached to the flower head of the Queen Anne's Lace.

Sideload a "Dark" mix, Antique Green + Celery Green + Charcoal Grey + Avocado 2:1:2:1, onto a no. 12 shader and walk a float at the base of the flower head stems. Sideload a no. 8 shader with the Dark mix and float it on the left, top and base of the main stem. Load a no. 10/0 liner with thinned Dark mix and pull additional stems on the left of the flower head. Sideload a no. 12 shader with a "Very Dark" mix of Avocado + Rookwood Red + Charcoal Grey 4:1:1, and deepen the already-established dark floats in the flower head. Use a no. 8 loaded with the Very Dark mix and deepen the floats on the stems.

6 Sideload a no. 8 shader with the Dark mix and float it at the base of each of the Queen Anne's Lace leaves. Then float it on the left side of the main stem. Sideload the Very Dark mix onto a no. 6 shader and deepen the previous floats.

7 Load a no. 10/0 liner with thinned Jade Green + Citron Green 1:2 and pull a light line on the right side of the stems in the Queen Anne's Lace flower head. Load a no. 10/0 liner with thinned "Highlight" mix, Limeade + Citron Green 1:1, and build up the floats on the stems and flower heads.

Sideload a no. 8 shader with the Light mix and float it on the right side of each of the leaves. Sideload a no. 6 shader with "Highlight" mix and float it within the previous Light floats. Repeat with floats of Limeade.

8 Use a no. 10 shader loaded with thinned Fleabane Flower Dark and add pink tints to the darker areas of the flower heads, stems and leaves. Use a no. 8 shader loaded with thinned Fleabane Very Dark and add some darker pink tints.

9 Load a no. 3 round fabric brush with Dark mix, Eggshell + Citron Green 1:1 and tap out the excess paint onto a waxed palette paper. Then stipple on the basic form of the head of the flowers. Load Medium Light Parchment on the brush and stipple it into the established flower head. Repeat the process with Light Buttermilk and then Highlight, Warm White.

10 Sideload a no. 10 shader with Fleabane Flower Medium and add pink tints to the large flower head and more pink tints to the smaller flower head. Then load thinned Fleabane Flower Dark and deepen some of the tints.

11 Load a no. 10/0 liner with Payne's Grey and base the bee's head and then pull the antennae and legs.

Load a ¼-inch (6mm) filbert rake with thinned mix of Primary Yellow + Warm White 1:1, and pull the yellow hairs of the mid-section of the bee body and add lighter hairs along the top of the middle area. Load thinned Milk Chocolate and add some darker hairs to the lower part.

Sideload a no. 4 shader with thinned Light mix and pull an elongated *C* stroke along the inside edge of each wing. Sideload a no. 4 shader with thinned Light Buttermilk and brighten the light areas on the wings. Sideload Very Dark and float it at the base of each wing and between the wings to separate them.

12 Load a ¼-inch (6mm) filbert rake with thinned Very Dark and pull dark hairs at the front and back of the bee. Load a no. 10/0 liner with thinned Very Dark and pull some dark hairs through the yellow section of the bee. Also, add very thin vein lines to the wings. Load a no. 10/0 liner with thinned Light and pull random hairs through the body.

13 Load a no. 12 shader with Medium mix, Celery Green + Antique Teal 6:1, and basecoat the chicory leaves and stems. Sideload a no. 10 shader with Dark and float it at the base of each leaf, then pull a back-to-back float through the center of the leaves to establish a shadow for the vein line. Add Dark to some of the leaf tips. Sideload Dark onto a no. 6 shader and float it at the top, bottom and along the left side of each stem. Deepen all of the previous floats with Very Dark mix, Antique Teal + Charcoal Grey 1:1, loaded on a no. 10 shader for the leaves and a no. 4 shader for the stems.

14 Sideload a no. 12 shader with Light mix, Jade Green + Antique Teal 14:1, and float it along the edges of the leaves. Reload the brush and use the chisel edge to pull a center vein line. Reload the brush with Light and use the chisel edge of the brush to add a light area to the right side of each stem. Use a no. 10 shader loaded with Highlight mix, Jade Green + Soft Sage 1:2, and repeat all the previous floats within the light areas.

Load a no. 10 shader with thinned Fleabane Flowers Medium and float some tints in the light to medium areas of the leaves.

15 Base each petal and bud with Chicory Flowers Medium mix, Countyry Blue + Soft Lilac 1:2, using a no. 4 shader. Sideload Dark onto a no. 8 shader and walk a float at the base of each petal and bud. Use a damp no. 4 filbert to stretch the lines created by the float. Deepen each of these floats with Very Dark mix, Country Blue + Payne's Grey 3:2, using a no. 6 shader.

16 Sideload Light, Soft Lilac, onto a no. 6 shader and make a back-to-back float in the center of each petal. Load a no. 10/0 liner with thinned Highlight, Blue Chiffon, and pull fine lines through the light area. Repeat the process with thinned 2nd Highlight, Cool White.

17 Load a no. 10/0 liner with PG + Fleabane Flower Very Dark 1:1 and add elongated dots to the center of each flower. Load a no. 10/0 liner with thinned Light and pull tiny lines from the top of each dot.

Sideload a no. 10 shader with thinned Fleabane Flower Medium and add some lighter pink tints to the chicory flowers.

18 Base the larger leaves using a no. 10 shader loaded with Fleabane Leaves & Stems Medium, Celery Green mix, Avocado + Celery Green + Charcoal Grey 2:2:1. Use a no. 10/0 liner for the stems and smaller leaves. Sideload Dark onto a no. 6 shader and float it at the top, base, along the left side of the stem and at the base of each leaf. Reload the brush and make a back-to-back float through the center of the larger leaves to establish a center vein line. Sideload a no. 6 shader with Very Dark mix, Evergreen + Charcoal Grey 1:1 and deepen the base of each leaf and the left side of each stem.

19 Sideload a no. 6 shader with Light, Limeade, and float it along the edges of the leaves and along the right side of each stem. Sideload Highlight mix, Warm white + Citron Green 1:1, onto a no. 6 shader and build up the highlight areas. Use a no. 6 filbert to blend.

20 Load a ¼-inch (6mm) filbert rake with thinned Fleabane Flowers Medium mix, Petal Pink + Rookwood Red 3:1, and pull short, curved lines that make up the flower petals. Load a no. 6 shader with Fleabane Flower mix, Vivid Violet + Rookwood Red 2:1, Dark and deepen the base of the petals around the center. Deepen the left side of each center further with a float of Very Dark, Rookwood Red.

Load thinned Light, Pink Chiffon, onto a no. 10/0 liner and pull random fine lines within the established petals.

21 Load a no. 3 round fabric brush with True Ochre and stipple the center of each opened flower. Sideload the brush with Milk Chocolate and deepen the left side and lower edge of each center.

Sideload the fabric brush with Primary Yellow and stipple a lighter area in the upper-right side of each center.

Sideload a no. 6 shader with thinned Chicory Flower Very Dark and add some blue tints to the fleabane flower petals.

22 Basecoat the wings with Butterflies Medium mix, Country Blue + Soft Lilac 1:1, using a no. 12 shader. Sideload Dark, Country Blue, onto a no. 10 shader and walk a float at the base of each wing. Use the chisel edge of a damp no. 6 filbert to stretch the float. Reload the brush and float Dark to separate the wings. Deepen each of the floats with Very Dark mix, Country Blue + Payne's Grey 1:1, using a no. 8 shader.

23 Sideload Light, Soft Lilac, onto a no. 12 shader and walk a float from the top edge to the base of each wing. Use the tips of a damp no. 6 filbert to stretch the float and pull the lines through the wing. Sideload Highlight, Blue Chiffon, onto a no. 10 shader and repeat the process. Sideload 2nd Highlight, Cool White, and repeat the floats only on the tip of the front wings.

24 Load a no. 10/0 liner with thinned Very Dark and add veins, dots and the fringing on the wing edges.

Sideload a no. 12 shader with thinned Fleabane Flower Medium and add some pink tints to the wings.

25 Load a no. 3 round with Medium and base the body of each butterfly. Load a ¼-inch (6mm) filbert rake with thinned Country Blue and add very fine, short hairs to the body. Load a no. 10/0 liner with thinned Payne's Grey and add some darker hairs along the bottom edge of the body and add the antennae.

Load a no. 10/0 liner brush with thinned Soft Lilac and add a few lighter hairs randomly through the body.

26 Apply a thin layer of plain glazing medium with a no. 10 sable bright to the lower fourth of the panel. Blot the same brush and then load it with a small amount of Olive Green and place it in the lower corners and along the bottom edge of the panel. Use a no. 6 sable filbert to blend.

27 Apply a small amount of Yellow Glaze on the bee, leaves and stems with a no.10 sable bright. Clean the brush and apply plain glazing medium to the flowers. Load a no. 6 sable flat with a small amount of Olive Green and place it in the darkest areas of each leaf, stem and Queen Anne's Lace flower head. Use a no. 6 sable filbert to blend. Load a no. 8 sable bright with Payne's Grey and deepen the dark areas of the butterfly and chicory. Deepen the base of the closed fleabane flowers and along the left side at the base of the open ones with a no. 8 sable bright loaded with Purple Madder Alizarin + Charcoal Grey. Load a no. 6 sable flat with Charcoal Grey and deepen the dark areas of the bee.

28 Sideload a no. 6 sable flat with warm white mix and re-highlight the butterfly and bee wings. Build up the highlights on all the flowers, leaves and stems with warm white mix. Use a no. 6 sable filbert to blend.

29 Sideload Purple Madder Alizarin on a no. 6 sable flat and brighten the tints on the Queen Anne's Lace and the leaves. Use a no. 6 sable filbert to blend.

TIN HEART
ORNAMENTS

These little ornaments will give you a chance to try out various techniques on designs that are not too complicated. Both have high-key value scales, meaning that the tones are within the high- (lightest) to medium-value scale. This limits the use of dark values to small amounts.

I have chosen a traditional subject with the mistletoe, and something a bit untraditional with the crocus. The mistletoe project has a lot of repetition with the leaves and berries, so it may be a good first choice for the beginning painter. The smooth mistletoe leaves allow you to concentrate on applying the floats and blending properly. For the crocus, we'll add the technique of "walking a float" to create a streaky or striped appearance on the flower petals. This technique is used multiple times throughout the remaining projects.

PATTERNS

These patterns may be hand-traced or photo-copied for personal use only.

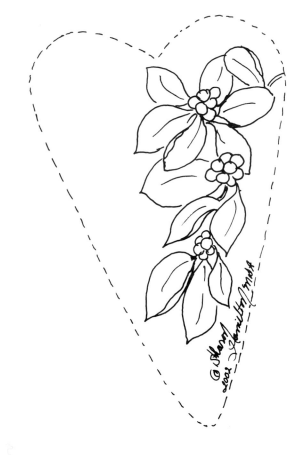

Mistletoe

Crocus

COLORS & MATERIALS

Antique Green
(DA)

Black Green
(DA)

Celery Green
(DA)

Charcoal Grey
(DA)

Cranberry Wine
(DA)

Jade Green
(DA)

Light
Buttermilk
(DA)

Light
Parchment
(DA)

Lilac
(DA)

Limeade
(DA)

Pink Chiffon
(DA)

Primary Yellow
(DA)

Summer Lilac
(DA)

True Ochre
(DA)

Vivid Violet
(DA)

Warm White
(DA)

Wild Orchid
(DA)

Cadmium
Yellow Pale
(WN)

Indian Yellow
(WN)

Olive Green
(WN)

Purple Madder
Alizarin
(WN)

Titanium White
(WN)

Warm White
mix
(See page 16)

SURFACE

Tin heart-shaped ornaments
from Painter's Paradise
(*See* Resource section)

PAINTS

DA = DecoArt
Americana Acrylics
WN = Winsor & Newton
Artists Oils

BRUSHES: LOEW-CORNELL

Comfort Series 3300 Shader
nos. 4, 6, 8, 10, 12, 14.
Comfort Series 3500 Filbert
nos. 6, 8. Comfort Series
3050 Script Liner no. 2.
Comfort Series Mid Length
Liner no. 10/0. Comfort
Series 3520 Filbert Rake
¼-inch (6mm). Arttec Red
Sable Series 124 Flat no. 6.
Arttec Red Sable Series 128
Filbert no. 6. Arttec Red
Sable Series 130B Bright
no. 8. Arttec Red Sable
Series 120 Round no. 1.
Comfort Series 3000 Round
no. 3. LaCorneille/Golden
Taklon Series JS Jackie Shaw
Liner no. 10/0. Arttec Red
Sable Series 124 Flat no. 6.
Arttec Red Series 128 Sable
Filbert nos. 4, 6.

ADDITIONAL SUPPLIES

Winsor & Newton Blending
& Glazing Medium.

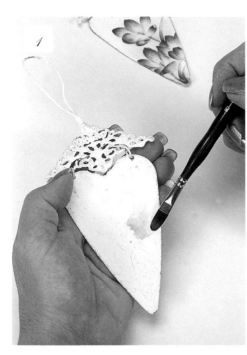

1 Transfer the pattern carefully onto the ornament surface using gray graphite paper. Sideload thinned Celery Green onto a no. 14 shader and float it behind the flowers and leaves. Use a damp no. 8 filbert to soften the outer edges of the floats so the background has a rouged appearance.

2 Load a no. 2 liner with a "Medium" mix of Jade Green + Light Parchment 1:1 and basecoat the leaves and stems.

3 Sideload a no. 4 shader with a "Dark" of Celery Green and walk a float at the base and tip of each leaf. Reload the brush and float it along the left side and at the base of each stem. Sideload into a "Very Dark" mix of Celery Green + Charcoal Grey + Black Green + Antique Green 4:1:1:1, and float it at the base of each stem and leaf.

4 Sideload a no. 4 shader with a "Light" of Limeade and walk a back-to-back float through the center of each leaf and along the right side of each stem.

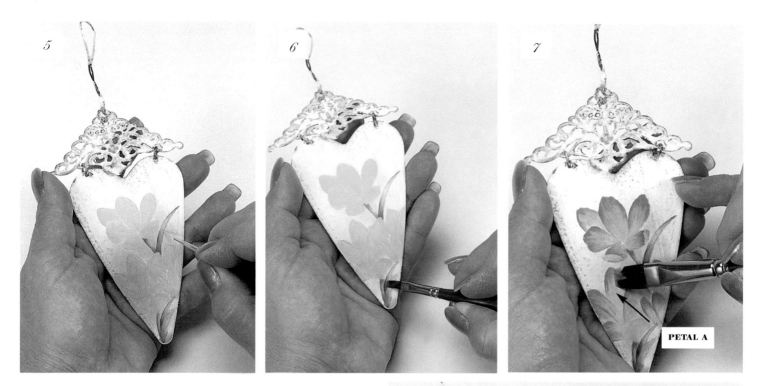

5 Load a no. 10/0 liner with a thinned "Highlight" of Warm White and add some lighter lines within the light areas of the leaves and stems.

6 Sideload thinned Wild Orchid on a no. 4 shader and float a purple tint at the top of each stem where it attaches to the flower. Sideload thinned Vivid Violet and add some tints to the dark areas of the leaves.

7 Load a no. 14 shader with the Medium mix and basecoat each of the petals. Sideload a no. 12 shader with a "Dark" of Summer Lilac and walk a float from the tip inward to the center of each petal with the exception of Petal A. Follow the petal contour while walking the float.

8 Use the chisel edge of a damp no. 8 filbert to stretch the lines of the walked float.

9

PETAL A

10

11

PETAL A

9 Float the "Dark" color, Summer Lilac, under the flipped petals and along the back edge of the flips with a no. 12 shader. Reload the brush and float along the top folded edge and left side of Petal A. Side-load a no. 10 shader with the "Very Dark" color, Wild Orchid, and repeat the floats within all of the previous Dark floats.

10 Use a damp no. 8 filbert to stretch the lines of the floats. Sideload a no. 8 shader with the "2nd Very Dark" color, Vivid Violet, and float it along the edges of the petal tips to darken them further.

11 Sideload the "Light" color, Pink Chiffon, onto a no. 12 shader and walk a float from the base toward the center of each petal. Use the tip of a damp no. 8 filbert to stretch the lines created by the float. Walk a float of the "Light" on the tip of Petal A and then use a no. 8 filbert to stretch the lines formed by the float.

12 Load a ¼-inch (6mm) filbert rake with the thinned "Light" and pull fine lines from the base toward the tip of each petal. Reload the brush and float it on the tips of the flipped petals.

12

13 Sideload the "Highlight" color, Warm White, on a no. 10 shader and walk floats within the previous "Light" floats.

14 Use a damp no. 6 filbert to stretch the ends of the floats.

15 Load a no. 10/0 liner with the thinned "Medium" color, Lilac, and pull fine, short stamen lines in the center of the crocus. Add random dots around the top of the stamens.

16 Load thinned "Dark" color, Summer Lilac, onto the liner and place it at the base and along the left side of each stamen. Place a bit of the "Dark" on the left side of each of the stamen dots.

17 Load the liner with the thinned "Light" color, Pink Chiffon, and add a highlight to each of the stamen dots.

18 Load a no. 6 sable flat with yellow glaze (see page 17) and apply it to the leaves and stems.

19 Sideload Olive Green onto a clean no. 6 sable flat and place it at the base of each stem and leaf.

20 Use a no. 6 sable filbert to blend the paint into the medium-value area.

21 Load a no. 1 sable round with Warm White mix (*see* page 16) and add a few streaks in the highlight areas of the leaves and stems.

Keep a separate brush for glazing unless otherwise indicated. It is best to keep a set of flat, bright and filbert brushes to apply and blend the dark values and dark tints. Likewise, it is best to keep a set of flat, bright and filbert brushes for the light values. This will keep the oil paint from becoming muddied when going from a very dark value to a very light value and vice versa.

22 Apply a thin layer of plain glazing medium to the crocus petals with a no. 6 sable flat.

23 Sideload Purple Madder Alizarin onto a no. 8 sable bright and place it in the dark tips of each petal and at the base of each stamen. Use a no. 4 sable filbert to blend.

24 Use a no. 8 sable bright and sideload it with Warm White mix. Place it at the base of each petal and pull it outward a little bit. Use a clean no. 6 sable filbert to blend.

25 Sideload a clean no. 6 sable flat with a very tiny amount of Indian Yellow and add yellow tints to the medium-to-light-value areas of some of the leaves and petals. Use a no. 6 sable filbert to blend.

1 Transfer the pattern carefully onto the ornament surface using gray graphite paper. Sideload thinned Cranberry Wine onto a no. 14 shader and float it behind the berries and leaves. Soften the outer edges of the floats with a damp no. 8 filbert so the background has a rouged appearance.

Load a no. 8 shader with a "Medium" mix of Jade Green + Light Parchment 1:1 and base each of the leaves.

2 Sideload a "Dark" of Celery Green onto a no. 6 shader and float it at the base of each leaf. Use a damp no. 6 filbert to soften the edge of the float. Reload the shader with the Dark color and make a back-to-back float through the center of each leaf to establish the center vein line. Reload and float it under the overlapping leaves and under the flipped edges to separate them from the body of the leaf. Sideload a no. 6 shader with a "Very Dark" mix of Celery Green + Black Green + Charcoal Grey + Antique Green 4:1:1:1 and deepen the previous dark floats. Use a damp no. 6 filbert to blend.

3 Sideload a no. 6 shader with a "Light" color of Limeade and float it on the edges of the leaves. Float it along the top edge of each flipped edge. Reload the brush and use the chisel edge to pull a center vein line through the leaf center.

4 Sideload a no. 4 shader with a "Highlight" mix of Limeade + Warm White mix 1:1 and float a lighter area within the previous "Light" floats and lighten the leaf veins.

5 Sideload thinned Cranberry Wine onto a no. 6 shader and float some pink tints on the edges of the leaves.

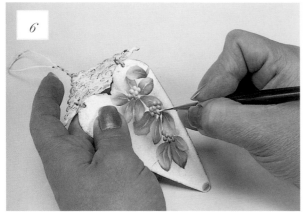

6 Load a no. 3 round brush with a "Medium" color, Light Parchment, and basecoat the berries. Sideload a "Dark" mix of Celery Green + True Ochre 3:1 onto a no. 4 shader and float it along the left edge of each berry. Sideload a "Very Dark" mix of Celery Green + Black Green + Charcoal Grey + Antique Green 4:1:1:1 onto the brush and deepen the "Dark" floats.

7 Sideload thinned Cranberry Wine onto a no. 4 shader and float pink tints along the left side of some of the berries.

Sideload a "Light" color of Light Buttermilk onto a no. 4 shader and float it around the right side of each berry. Load a no. 10/0 liner with a "Highlight" color, Warm White, and add a dot of highlight to the lightest berries.

8 Apply a thin layer of plain glazing medium to the leaves with a no. 6 sable flat. Sideload a small amount of Olive Green onto a no. 6 sable flat and place it at the base of each leaf. Use a no. 6 sable filbert to blend.

9 Deepen the tints on the leaves and berries with a bit of Purple Madder Alizarin using a no. 6 sable flat. Blend the paint with a no. 6 sable filbert.

Sideload a small amount of Warm White mix (*see* page 16) onto a clean no. 6 sable flat and place it within the highlight area of each leaf. Use a clean no. 6 sable filbert to blend. Load a no. 1 sable round with Warm White mix and place a highlight within each berry.

Oops! When placing the oil paint, be careful not to use too much paint. It will make it difficult to blend properly. When blending, be sure not to leave a dark ridge of paint. It should be blended smoothly and still show gradation between the values.

DAYLILIES SPICE BIN

I have always loved daylilies. They are in just about every garden that I have around my home! They come in almost any color of the rainbow. I planted these lovely yellow and green ones this summer, and when they bloomed, they were absolutely gorgeous. I photographed them because I knew that I just had to paint them!

I've chosen to incorporate a faux finish in this project to break up the large expanse of space on the spice bin and enhance the design. The gold used in the faux finish and on the trim accents the yellow and green daylilies nicely.

To develop your technical skills, you will learn to paint long, thin petals that radiate out from the throat of the flower. The petals are painted by working through the various values, and then the throat is developed through a series of yellow-green floats that match the underlying values of the petals.

PATTERN

This pattern may be hand-traced or photo-copied for personal use only.

COLORS & MATERIALS

Celery Green
(DA)

Citron Green
(DA)

Charcoal Grey
(DA)

Cool White
(DA)

Eggshell
(DA)

Plantation Pine
(DA)

Plum
(DA)

Taffy Cream
(DA)

Taupe
(DA)

Warm White
(DA)

Yellow Light
(DA)

Glorious Gold
(DM)

Cadmium
Yellow Pale
(WN)

Charcoal Grey
(WN)

Indian Yellow
(WN)

Olive Green
(WN)

Purple Madder
Alizarin
(WN)

Titanium White
(WN)

Warm White
mix (WN)
(*See* page 16)

SURFACE

Metal spice bin from
Painter's Paradise
(*See* Resource section)

PAINTS

DA = DecoArt
Americana Acrylics
DM = DecoArt Dazzling
Metallics
WN = Winsor & Newton
Artists Oils

BRUSHES: LOEW-CORNELL

Comfort Series 3550
Glaze/Wash 1/2-inch
(12mm), 1-inch (25mm).
Comfort Series 3300 Shader
nos. 4, 6, 8, 10, 12, 14.
Comfort Series 3500 Filbert
nos. 6, 8, 10. Comfort Series
3050 Script Liner no. 1.
Comfort Series 3320 Mid
Length Liner no. 10/0.
Arttec Red Sable Series 124
Flat nos. 2, 6, 8. Arttec Red
Sable Series 128 Filbert nos.
6, 8. Arttec Red Sable Series
130B Bright nos. 8, 10.
Arttec Red Sable Series 120
Round no. 1.

ADDITIONAL SUPPLIES

Winsor & Newton Blending
& Glazing Medium. plastic
wrap. DecoArt Faux Glazing
Medium. DecoArt Multi-
Purpose Sealer. Krylon
18Kt. Gold Leafing Pen.

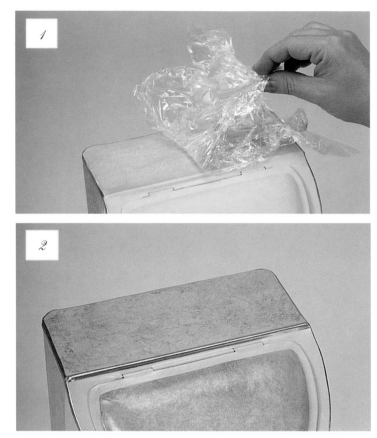

1 Base the bin with Eggshell + sealer 1:1, using a 1-inch (25mm) wash brush. Then when it is dry, apply a second coat on the front of the bin. Transfer the oval with white graphite paper. Load a 1-inch wash brush with a mix of Celery Green + Faux Glazing Medium 1:2, and apply it to the oval. Lay a piece of wrinkled plastic wrap into the wet glaze and lift. While it's drying, repeat the process on the lid, top, back and sides of the bin.

2 Mix the background "Dark" mix, Celery Green + Plantation Pine + Charcoal Grey 6:3:2, with Faux Glazing Medium 1:2 and dip a piece of crumpled plastic wrap into it. Tap the plastic wrap onto a piece of palette paper and then tap it onto the oval area of the bin. Reload the plastic wrap in the same way and apply it to the other glazed areas of the bin. Load clean plastic wrap with Glorious Gold + Faux Glazing Medium 1:5 and tap it over all the glazed areas to complete them.

When the glaze is fully dry, apply the pattern with graphite paper.

3 Base each of the petals with the petal "Medium" mix, Taupe + Cool White (1:1), using a 1/2-inch (12mm) wash brush. Sideload the petal "Dark" mix, Taupe + Plum (3:1), onto the brush and walk a float close to the outer edge of each petal. Use a damp no. 10 filbert to stretch and pull the lines formed by the walked float. Reload the brush and walk a float on both sides of where the center vein would be, leaving the center open. Float the Dark mix under any flipped petals.

4 Sideload the petal "Very Dark" mix, Plum + Taupe + Plantation Pine 3:2:1, onto a no. 14 shader and deepen the previous dark floats. Use a no. 8 filbert to blend.

If you leave a little space between the petals when basecoating the flower, you can easily erase the graphite lines when the base color has dried. Then when you float the values onto each petal, float over the open space and close it up.

5 Sideload the petal "Light" mix, Warm White + Taupe 5:1, onto a no. 14 shader and walk a float in the light areas of each petal. Use a damp no. 8 filbert to pull and stretch the lines from the float to follow the contour of the petal. Float the Light mix on the tips of the flipped edges. Using a no. 10 shader, reload the brush and use the chisel edge to pull a light area through the center vein line of the petals. Sideload the petal "Highlight" color, Warm White mix, onto a no. 10 shader and walk a lighter float within the established light areas. Use a damp no. 6 filbert to stretch the lines of the float. Reload the shader with Warm White and build up the light within each center vein.

6 Sideload a ¹/₂-inch (12mm) wash brush with a thinned throat "Highlight" color of Taffy Cream and float it at the base of the throat. Use a damp no. 10 filbert and pull the soft edge of the float about a third of the way into the body of the petal. Sideload the brush with thinned throat "Light" color, Yellow Light, and float it on top of the previous float. Use the damp filbert to stretch the yellow outward. Sideload the throat "Medium" color, Citron Green, onto a no. 14 shader and float it within the Light area while still allowing the yellow to show through. Deepen the base of the throat with a float of the throat "Dark" mix, Citron Green + Plantation Pine 2:1, using a no. 12 shader.

7 Load a no. 1 liner with thinned pistil-and-stamen "Medium" mix, Taffy Cream + Celery Green + Citron Green 2:1:1, and pull a gently curved line for each pistil and stamen. Add a cluster of three dots to the end of the pistil. Sideload the pistil-and-stamen "Dark" mix, Citron Green + Plantation Pine + Plum 2:3:1, onto a no. 4 shader and float it at the end of each pistil and stamen. Reload the brush and float it along the left side of the dot cluster.

Load a no. 10/0 liner with thinned pistil-and-stamen "Light" mix, Medium mix + Warm White 1:1, and add a light area in the center of each pistil.

8 Load a no. 4 shader with the stamen-end "Medium" mix, Yellow Light + Plum 6:1, and base each of the stamen ends. Sideload stamen-end "Dark" mix, Yellow Light + Plum 2:1, onto the brush and float it along the left side and lower edge of each stamen end. Sideload the stamen-end "Very Dark" mix, Plum + Plantation Pine 6:1, and deepen the floats at the base of each stamen end.

Load a no. 10/0 liner with thinned stamen-end "Light" mix, Yellow Light + Taffy Cream + Plum 8:2:1, and stipple in the light area along the right side of each stamen end.

9 Base each stem and bud with stem-and-bud "Medium" mix, Celery Green + Citron Green 2:1, using a no. 10 shader. Sideload stem-and-bud "Dark" mix, Celery Green + Citron Green + Plantation Pine 1:1:1 onto a no. 10 shader and float it along the left side and base of each bud and stem. Reload the brush and float under the overlapped bud. Sideload a no. 6 shader with the Dark mix and make a back-to-back float through the center of each bud. Sideload the no. 8 shader with the stem-and-bud "Very Dark" mix, Plantation Pine + Plum 6:1, and deepen the base of each bud and stem.

10 Sideload the petal "Very Dark" mix, Plum + Taupe + Plantation Pine 3:2:1, onto a no. 10 shader and float a tint along the left side and base of each bud.

11 Sideload a no. 6 shader with stem-and-bud "Light" mix, Citron Green + Taffy Cream (1:1) and float it at the top, left and right edge of each bud. Use a damp no. 6 filbert to soften the floats.

Repeat the floats on the right side of the bud. Use a no. 10/0 liner brush loaded with the Light mix to add a light area to the center of each stem.

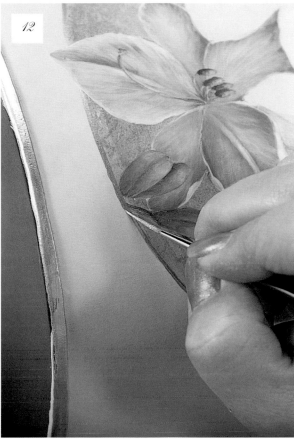

12 Load a no. 1 liner with thinned Glorious Gold and pull a fine line around the oval inset.

13 The gold leafing must be applied after the painting has been varnished. Shake the 18Kt. Gold Leafing Pen well. Press the tip onto palette paper until the paint permeates the tip. Carefully place the tip of the pen on the edge of the tin and gently pull it along.

Use the pen to apply gold leafing to the raised rims of the bin.

If you don't own sable brushes for the oil glazing, go ahead and use clean, dry acrylic brushes. Be sure to clean them thoroughly after the oil glazing stage to remove any oil residue before using them for acrylics again.

Conversion: Loew-Cornell Comfort Series 3300 shader no. 10 = Loew-Cornell Arttec Red Sable Series 130B Bright no. 8

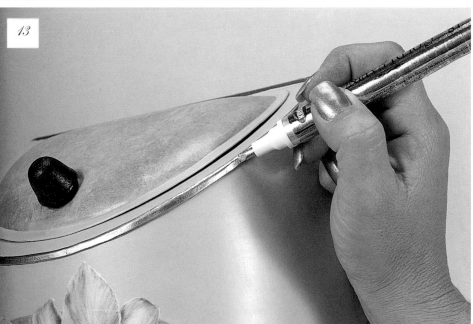

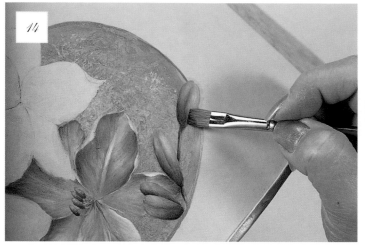

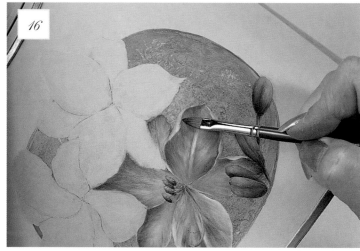

14 Apply a thin layer of yellow glaze (see page 17) to the stems and buds with a no. 10 sable bright. Apply a thin layer of plain glazing medium to the flowers. Use a clean no. 6 sable flat and place a small amount of Olive Green at the base of each bud and along the left side of each stem. Use a no. 6 sable filbert to blend the paint.

Deepen the dark areas on the petals with Purple Madder Alizarin using a no. 8 sable bright. Take a no. 6 sable filbert and blend. Deepen the darkest areas a bit with Charcoal Grey (WN). Blend with a no. 6 sable filbert.

15 Sideload a very tiny amount of Indian Yellow onto a no. 8 sable bright and add a yellow tint in each lily throat. Use a no. 6 sable filbert to blend. Sideload a no. 8 sable bright with Purple Madder Alizarin and add a pink tint to the base of each of the buds. Blend the tints with a no. 8 sable filbert.

16 Sideload a small amount of Warm White mix onto a no. 8 sable flat and place it in the lightest area of each petal, bud and stem. Blend with a no. 6 filbert. Add highlights to the ends of the pistils and stamens with Warm White mix loaded on a no. 6 sable flat.

17 Load a no. 1 sable round with a small amount of Charcoal Grey (WN) + a tiny amount of Olive Green. Add cast shadows from the pistils and stamens onto the lily petals. Sideload Purple Madder Alizarin onto a no. 2 sable flat and deepen the left side of each stamen.

YELLOW TULIPS
MAIL KEEPER

Tulips are one of my favorite subjects to paint! With so many colors and shapes, they are an endless source of inspiration to me. This design began with a photo that I had taken of some irresistible yellow tulips. I knew right away that they would work beautifully on this unusual tin mail keeper.

Tulips have some different qualities to them. The leaves are smooth and shiny to the point of having an almost waxy look. The petals have center vein lines and a lot of flipped edges, much like a leaf. I added a little tint of red to the tips of the petals to add interest.

You will learn to use a filbert rake to add very fine textural side-veins to the tulips so they will appear more realistic. Gold leafing is added to enhance the warm tones of the tulips.

This project incorporates thin washes over the leaves to warm them up and adjust the overall temperature.

PATTERN

This pattern may be hand-traced or photocopied for personal use only. Enlarge at 153% to bring it up to full size

COLORS & MATERIALS

Buttermilk
(DA)

Celery Green
(DA)

Charcoal Grey
(DA)

Honey Brown
(DA)

Light
Buttermilk
(DA)

Limeade
(DA)

Marigold
(DA)

Pineapple
(DA)

Plantation Pine
(DA)

Primary Yellow
(DA)

Rookwood Red
(DA)

Soft Black
(DA)

Titanium White
(DA)

True Ochre
(DA)

Yellow Green
(DA)

Yellow Light
(DA)

Alizarin
Crimson
(WN)

Cadmium
Yellow Pale
(WN)

Charcoal Grey
(WN)

Indian Yellow
(WN)

Olive Green
(WN)

Titanium White
(WN)

Warm White
mix (WN)
(*See* page 16)

SURFACE

Tin mail keeper from
Painter's Paradise
(*See* Resource section.)

PAINTS

DA = DecoArt
Americana Acrylics
WN = Winsor & Newton
Artists Oils

BRUSHES: LOEW-CORNELL

Comfort Series 3550
Glaze/Wash 3/4-inch (19mm),
1/2-inch (12mm) Wash.
Comfort Series 3300 Shader
nos. 4, 6, 8, 10, 12, 14.
Comfort Series 3500 Filbert
nos. 2, 8, 10. Comfort Series
3520 Filbert Rake 1/4-inch
(6mm). Comfort Series Mid
Length Liner no. 10/0.
Arttec Red Sable Series 124
Flat no. 6. Arttec Red Sable
Series 126 Filbert nos. 4, 6.
Arttec Red Sable Series 130B
Bright nos. 8, 10. Arttec Red
Sable Series 120 Round no. 1.

ADDITIONAL SUPPLIES

Winsor & Newton Blending
& Glazing Medium. Krylon
18Kt. Gold Leafing Pen

1 Transfer the pattern with white graphite paper. Base the leaves using a 3/4-inch (19mm) wash brush loaded with the "Medium" mix, Celery Green + Plantation Pine 2:1.

Sideload the "Dark" mix, Plantation Pine + Celery Green + Charcoal Grey (DA) 4:2:1, onto a no. 14 shader. Float it at the base of each leaf. Reload the brush and pull a back-to-back float through the center of each leaf to establish a shadow for the vein line. Use a damp no. 8 filbert to blend the floats. Reload the no. 14 shader and float the Dark mix along the back edge and under each flipped area. Float the same mix along the top, bottom and left side of each stem. Sideload a no. 14 shader with the "Very Dark" mix, Plantation Pine + Charcoal Grey (DA) + Soft Black 7:1:2, and repeat the previous floats to deepen them. Sideload the shader with the "2nd Very Dark" mix, Plantation Pine + Soft Black 2:1, and deepen the floats at the base of the leaves.

2 Wash a glaze of thinned Yellow Green over the leaves and stems with a 3/4-inch (19mm) wash brush.

3 Sideload a no. 14 shader with the "Light" mix, Limeade + Pineapple + Yellow Light 2:1:1, and float it on the edges of the leaves and along the stems to establish the light areas. Use a damp no. 10 filbert to blend the edges of the float. Reload the shader with the Light mix and use the chisel edge to pull the center vein line. Sideload a no. 12 shader with the "Highlight" mix, Limeade + Pineapple 2:1, and float it within the previous light floats. Sideload the 2nd Highlight color, Limeade, onto a no. 10 shader and float it only in the lightest areas of the leaves. Use a damp no. 8 filbert to blend the floats.

4 Load a no. 14 shader with thinned Yellow Light and wash it over the leaves and stems.

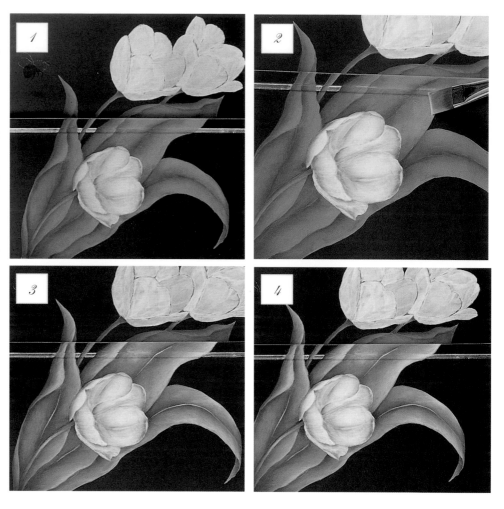

If needed, build up the 2nd Highlight and 2nd Very Dark floats again.

5 You will first paint the bottom and the upper right tulips. Load a 1/2-inch (12mm) wash brush and basecoat these two tulips with the "Medium" mix, Pineapple + Yellow Light 4:1. Sideload the brush with the "Dark" color, Primary Yellow, and float it at the base of each petal and underneath each flip. Reload the brush and pull a back-to-back float through the center of the veined petals. Use a damp filbert to stretch the edges of the float. Sideload a no. 12 shader with the "Very Dark" color, Honey Brown, and deepen all the previous floats. Sideload the brush with the "2nd Very Dark" mix, True Ochre + Plantation Pine + Charcoal Grey 5:2:1, and deepen the floats in the darkest areas of the tulips.

6 Sideload a no. 14 shader with the "Light" color, Buttermilk, and walk a float in the light area of each petal. Reload the brush and use the chisel edge to pull a vein line through the center of the petal.

Load a 1/4-inch (6mm) filbert rake with thinned "Highlight" color, Light Buttermilk, and pull some tiny lines on the petals to give them texture.

Sideload a no. 10 shader with the "2nd Highlight" color, Titanium White, and float it in the lightest areas of the tulip petals.

7 Sideload a 1/2-inch (12mm) wash brush with thinned Rookwood Red and float red tints on the leaves and petals. Use a no. 10 filbert to blend the floats. Load a no.10 shader with thinned Rookwood Red and walk a float in the *V* areas of the tulip petals.

Basecoat the remaining tulip using a 1/2-inch (12mm) wash brush loaded with the "Medium" mix, Pineapple + Yellow Light + Celery Green 4:2:1,. Sideload the brush with the "Dark" mix, True Ochre + Celery Green 4:1, and float it at the base of each petal and underneath each flip. Reload the brush and pull a back-to-back float through the center of the veined petals. Use a damp filbert to stretch the edges of the float. Sideload a no. 12 shader with the "Very Dark" mix, True Ochre + Plantation Pine + Charcoal Grey (DA) 5:2:1, and deepen all the previous floats on the third tulip

Sideload a no. 14 shader with the "Light" color, Buttermilk, and walk a float in the light area of each petal. Reload and use the chisel edge to pull a vein line through the center of the petal.

Load a 1/4-inch (6mm) filbert rake with thinned Highlight color, Light Buttermilk, and pull some very tiny lines on the petals to give them texture.

Sideload a 1/2-inch (12mm) wash brush with thinned Rookwood Red and float red tints on the petals. Use a no. 10 filbert to blend. Load a no. 10 shader with thinned Rookwood Red and walk a float in the V areas of the tulip petals.

8 Use a no. 10/0 liner with thinned "Medium" mix, Celery Green + Yellow Light + Pineapple 1:2:1, and basecoat the stamens and pistils. Sideload a no. 4 shader with the "Dark" mix, Yellow Light + Celery Green 4:1, and float the dark areas of the pistils and stamens.

Load a no. 10/0 liner with thinned "Light" color, Pineapple, and pull a light line through the center of each stamen. Use the tip of the liner to tap on the light areas at the end of the pistil.

Sideload the "Very Dark" mix, True Ochre + Plantation Pine + Charcoal Grey (DA) 5:2:1 onto a no. 4 shader and float it underneath the top sections of the pistil, and deepen the center of the pistil.

9 Load a no. 2 filbert with the stamen-end "Dark" color, Honey Brown, and work out the excess paint onto the palette. Use the tips of the brush to tap on each stamen end. Load the brush with Very Dark mix and tap it along the left side of the stamen.

Load the filbert with the "Medium" color, Marigold, and tap it along the right side of each stamen. Repeat the process with the "Light" color, Yelow Light, and then the "Highlight" color, Pineapple.

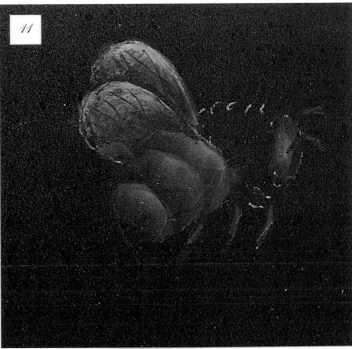

10 Basecoat the bumble bee body and head with the "Dark" color, Soft Black, loaded on a no. 4 shader. Load a no. 10/0 liner with thinned Dark color and pull the legs and antennae. Sideload the "Medium" color, Charcoal Grey (DA), on a no. 6 shader and float a series of crescent shapes on the lower part of the body. Reload and float the color on the lower part of the head. Use a no. 10/0 liner loaded with the same color and add some lighter areas to the legs. Sideload the "Light" mix, Pineapple + Charcoal Grey (DA) 1:2 onto a no. 6 shader and float it within each of the Medium-color floats.

11 Sideload a no. 8 shader with the Dark color, Soft Black, and float it on the underside of each wing.

Sideload the brush with the Light mix and float it along the top edge of the wing. Sideload thinned Pineapple and build up the tip of each wing.

Load a no. 10/0 liner with thinned Dark color and pull a line around the top of each wing; pull fine vein lines through each wing.

12 Load a 1/4-inch (6mm) filbert rake with thinned Marigold and pull yellow hairs that form the round, upper portion of the bee body. Load the rake with thinned Yellow Light and add some lighter hairs. Load the rake with thinned Soft Black and add the dark hairs within the yellow area. Then add the lightest hairs with thinned Pineapple. Sideload a no. 6 shader and float thinned Honey Brown along the left side of the yellow hairy section. Sideload Rookwood Red onto a no. 10 shader and float a tint on the bee body.

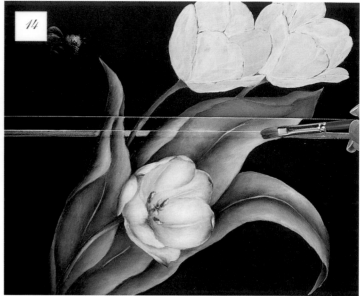

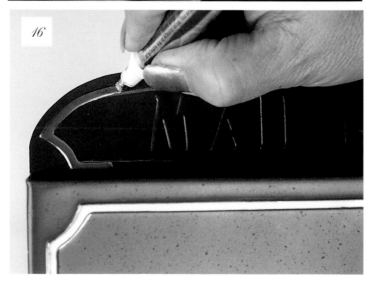

13 Apply yellow glaze (see page 17) to the bee, petals, leaves and stems with a no. 8 sable bright. Sideload Olive Green onto a no. 10 sable bright and place it in the darkest areas of the leaves and stems. Use a no. 6 sable filbert to stretch and blend the paint. Load a no. 10 sable bright with Charcoal Grey (WN) and place it in the darkest areas of the tulip petals. This is just a hint of color. Use a no. 6 sable filbert to blend. Place Charcoal Grey (WN) on the back end and underside of the bee and blend with the filbert.

14 Sideload Warm White mix (*see* page 16) onto a no. 6 sable flat and place it in the lightest area of each leaf, stem, and tulip petal, as well as in the front portion of the bee and on the tips of the bee wings. Use a no.6 filbert to stretch and blend the paint.

15 Sideload Alizarin Crimson onto a no. 6 sable flat and brighten the red tints on the tulips. Add a cast shadow to the left of the bottom tulip stem and soften it with a filbert.
    Add cast shadows with Charcoal Grey (WN) loaded on a no. 1 sable round to the left of the stamens in the bottom tulip. Blend them with a no. 4 sable filbert.

16 Use the 18Kt. Gold Leafing Pen to apply gold accents on the raised edges of the letter holder. (Refer to the Daylilies Spice Bin project for detailed instructions.)

WISTERIA TRAY

These lovely clusters of wisteria hang down gracefully from my garden arbor each summer. I particularly enjoy the peacefulness that they impart with their delicate violet blossoms.

In this lesson you will learn yet another background treatment. The overall background is a solid dark green, with several other values and hues of green slip-slapped into one another to create depth. The illusion is that of additional leaves appearing to be out of focus in the background. The next layer is made up of dark leaves with limited values and not much detail. They help to support the main leaves, which are very detailed with lots of values. These main leaves, in turn, support the wisteria flowers and create flow within the design.

Wisteria is quite different from other flower types. Each blossom is made up of three petals, the top one being most prominent, with a wash of buttery yellow in its center. This main petal also has an unusual *U*-shaped center, and the petal seems to ripple around it.

I hope that you will enjoy painting this enchanting wisteria as much as I have enjoyed sharing it with you!

This project incorporates thin washes over the leaves to warm them up and adjust the overall temperature.

PATTERN

This pattern
may be
hand-traced
or photo-
copied for
personal
use only.
Enlarge at
200% to
bring it up
to full size.

COLORS & MATERIALS

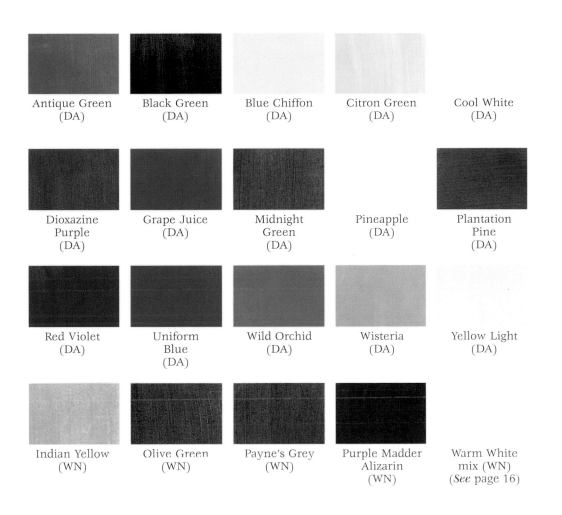

Antique Green (DA)

Black Green (DA)

Blue Chiffon (DA)

Citron Green (DA)

Cool White (DA)

Dioxazine Purple (DA)

Grape Juice (DA)

Midnight Green (DA)

Pineapple (DA)

Plantation Pine (DA)

Red Violet (DA)

Uniform Blue (DA)

Wild Orchid (DA)

Wisteria (DA)

Yellow Light (DA)

Indian Yellow (WN)

Olive Green (WN)

Payne's Grey (WN)

Purple Madder Alizarin (WN)

Warm White mix (WN) (*See* page 16)

SURFACE

17-inch Scooped Plate by Barb Watson's Brushworks (*See* Resource section)

PAINTS

DA = DecoArt Americana Acrylics
WN = Winsor & Newton Artists Oils

BRUSHES: LOEW–CORNELL

Comfort Series 3550 Glaze/Wash 1–inch (25mm). Comfort Series 3300 Shader nos. 4, 6, 8, 10, 12. Comfort Series 3500 Filbert no. 8. Comfort Series Script Liner no. 1. Comfort Series 3370 Mid Length Liner no. 10/0. Arttec Red Sable Series 124 Flat no. 6. Arttec Red Sable Series 128 Filbert no. 6. Arttec Red Sable Series 130B Bright nos. 8, 10.

ADDITIONAL SUPPLIES

Winsor & Newton Blending & Glazing Medium. DecoArt Multi-Purpose Sealer.

1

1 Basecoat the plate with Black Green + sealer, using a 1-inch (25mm) wash brush; repeat for good coverage. Sideload the flat with thinned Midnite Green and slip-slap it in the area under the design. While it is still wet, sideload Plantation Pine and slip-slap it within the Black Green area. Sideload Antique Green and slip-slap it within a smaller area. Reload the brush and pull some strokes that vaguely resemble the shape of the leaves. Then add an even lighter area with Citron Green. Allow the green values to dry and then add some purple tints with thinned Dioxazine Purple. When dry, transfer the main lines of the patterns with white graphite.

2 Base the under-leaves with a "Medium" mix of Antique Green + Midnite Green 1:1, using a no. 12 shader. Sideload a no. 10 shader with a "Dark" of Midnite Green and float it at the base of each leaf. Reload the brush and make a back-to-back float through the center of the leaf to establish a shadow for the vein line.

Basecoat the top leaves with a "Medium" of Antique Green, using a no. 12 shader. Sideload the "Dark" mix, Antique Green + Dioxazine Purple + Plantation Pine 1:1:1, onto a no. 12 shader and float it at the base of each leaf and under any flips. Reload the brush and make a back-to-back float to establish the shadow for the center vein line.

Sideload a "Very Dark" of Red Violet on a no. 10 shader, and repeat the floats within the dark areas of the under-leaves and the top leaves.

3 Sideload a "Light" of Antique Green, onto a no. 10 shader and float it along the edges of the under-leaves. Use a no. 8 filbert to blend the float. Reload the shader and use the chisel edge to pull the center vein line.

The under-leaves are merely supporting the design and should remain dark and in the background.

Where the end of the flip tapers off into the leaf, it's best to use a liner brush loaded with Citron Green to connect that point to the edge of the leaf.

4 Sideload a no. 12 shader with the "Light" mix of Citron Green + Antique Green 2:1. Walk a float along the edge of each leaf and the flipped edges of the top leaves. Use a no. 8 filbert to stretch the floats if needed. Repeat floats on the left side of the leaves. Reload the shader and use the chisel edge to pull the center vein line. Sideload a no. 10 shader with the "Highlight" color, Citron Green, and repeat the floats. Use a no. 8 filbert to blend. Sideload the "2nd Highlight" mix, Citron Green + Pineapple 1:1, onto a no. 8 shader and float it only on the left highlighted side of the leaves.

5 Base the darker buds and lower parts of the blossoms using a no. 6 shader with a "Medium" of Wild Orchid. Base the lighter buds with a "Light" of Wisteria.
  Sideload a "Dark" of Grape Juice onto a no. 4 shader and float it at the base of the buds. Sideload "Dark" onto a no. 10 shader and float it along the bottom edge of each lower petal. Float between the two petals to separate them. Deepen the darkest buds with an additional float of "Very Dark", Uniform Blue, with a no. 8 shader.

6 Sideload thinned Dioxazine Purple + Red Violet 1:1, and wash it over the back string of buds with a no. 10 shader.

7 Float the same mix along the base of each of the dark lower petals with a no. 10 shader.

8 Sideload the "Light", Wisteria, onto a no. 4 shader and float it at the tip of each bud. Sideload a no. 12 shader with "Light" and walk a float at the base of each petal. Sideload a no. 8 shader and float Blue Chiffon in the lightest areas.

9 Load a no. 12 shader and basecoat each of the top petals with the "Medium", Wisteria. Sideload a "Light" of Blue Chiffon onto a no. 10 shader and walk a float around the outside edge of each petal. Sideload a "Highlight" of Cool White onto a no. 10 shader and float it along the tip and outside edge of each petal. Sideload a no. 10 shader with "Highlight" and float it along the tips and right edges.

10 Sideload a "Dark" of Wild Orchid onto a no. 10 shader and float it at the base of each petal and under any flipped areas

11 Sideload a "Very Dark" of Uniform Blue onto a no. 8 shader and deepen each of the previous floats.

12 Sideload "Light" onto a no. 6 shader and float it in a *U* shape that makes up the center of the petal. Sideload Yellow Light onto a no. 6 shader and float it at the base of the *U*-shaped center. Deepen the base of each center with Yellow Light + Red Violet 4:1.

13 Sideload "Very Dark" onto a no. 8 shader and float it behind each *U* to separate it from the petal.

14 Load a no. 1 liner with thinned "Medium" leaf mix of Antique Green and pull graceful lines for the tendrils. Load a no. 10/0 liner with a "Very Dark" of Red Violet and deepen each end and the underside of each tendril.

Load a no. 10/0 liner with thinned "Light" mix of Citron Green + Antique Green 2:1, and place it in the light areas of each of the tendrils.

15 Apply plain glazing medium to the under-leaves, blossoms and buds. Apply Yellow Glaze (see page 17) on all remaining elements using a no. 10 sable bright.

Sideload Olive Green + Payne's Grey on a no. 8 sable bright and place it in the darkest area of each of the under-leaves. Sideload Olive Green onto a no. 8 sable bright and deepen the dark areas on all of the remaining leaves and stems. Use a no. 6 sable filbert to blend.

Sideload a no. 6 sable flat with Purple Madder Alizarin and deepen the bases of the small buds.

Sideload a no. 6 sable flat with Payne's Grey and deepen each of the darkest areas on the flowers and the large buds. Use a no. 6 sable filbert to blend.

16 Add some tints to the edges and to the sides of some of the leaves with Purple Madder Alizarin. Sideload a clean no. 6 sable flat with Warm White mix (*see* page 16) and build up the highlights on the top leaves, petals and buds. Blend with a no. 6 sable filbert.

Sideload a no. 6 sable flat with Purple Madder Alizarin and add tints to the edges of some of the leaves. Use a no. 6 sable filbert to blend. Add Indian Yellow tints to the flower centers and blend with a no. 6 sable filbert.

Don't worry about getting glaze onto the background of your project. It will dry and will disappear after it's been varnished.

DOGWOOD BOX

My white dogwood is one of the most enchanting trees in my gardens. I walked outside late one afternoon this spring and saw how the warm afternoon sunlight was softly illuminating the flowers. I raced inside for my camera so I could catch the light before the sun went down. The warm colors of the flower were so stunning against the blue-green background that I knew, before I snapped the shutter, that I would be sharing this lovely flower in a future painting project.

The ridged texture of the dogwood petals in this project is created with the technique of walked and stretched floats. The leaves also have texture and detail. The center of the dogwood blossom is unusual, with little round stamens and miniature flowers blooming within it.

This lesson adds another technique, with the unusual treatment of the background. My slip-slap method of applying the paint, in what appears to be an almost haphazard style, re-creates the look of the out-of-focus background generally seen in photos. I chose to apply rice paper to the sides of the box to add some textural interest to it.

PATTERN

This pattern may be hand-traced or photocopied for personal use only. Reduce 62% before using.

COLORS & MATERIALS

Antique Green
(DA)

Blue Chiffon
(DA)

Burnt Sienna
(DA)

Buttermilk
(DA)

Citron Green
(DA)

Cranberry
Wine
(DA)

French
Grey Blue
(DA)

French Vanilla
(DA)

Jade Green
(DA)

Light
Buttermilk
(DA)

Milk Chocolate
(DA)

Moon Yellow
(DA)

Plantation Pine
(DA)

Primary Yellow
(DA)

Rookwood Red
(DA)

Uniform Blue
(DA)

Warm White
(DA)

Winter Blue
(DA)

Alizarin
Crimson
(WN)

Cadmium
Yellow Pale
(WN)

Charcoal Grey
(WN)

Indian Yellow
(WN)

Olive Green
(WN)

Titanium White
(WN)

Warm White
mix (WN)
(*See* page 16)

SURFACE

Tea box by Wood Concepts
(*See* Resource section)

PAINTS

DA = DecoArt
Americana Acrylics
WN = Winsor & Newton
Artists Oils

BRUSHES: LOEW–CORNELL

Comfort Series 3550
Glaze/Wash 3/4-inch (19mm),
1-inch (25mm). Comfort
Series 3300 Shader nos. 2, 4,
6, 8, 10, 12, 14. Comfort
Series 3500 Filbert nos. 6, 8,
10. Comfort Series 3520 1/4-
inch (6mm) Filbert Rake
Comfort Series 3000 Round
no. 3. Comfort Series 3320
Mid–Length Liner no. 10/0.
Arttec Red Sable Series 124
Flat nos. 4, 6,. Arttec Red
Sable Series 128 Filbert nos.
4, 6. Arttec Red Sable Series
130B Bright no. 10.

ADDITIONAL SUPPLIES

DecoArt Multi-Purpose
Sealer. Winsor & Newton
Blending & Glazing Medium.
Rice paper or tissue paper.

1 Cut a piece of rice paper to fit the section between the routed edges of the lower part of the box. Allow the rice paper edges to overlap approximately 1 inch (25mm) where they meet. Apply a thin layer of sealer to one section of the box and to one side of the rice paper with a 3/4-inch (19mm) wash brush.

2 Position the precut paper onto the wet surface and smooth it down a bit with the 1-inch (25mm) flat brush loaded with sealer. Allow some of the wrinkles to remain for the desired effect. Continue this process until the entire box is covered. After the rice paper is completely dry, basecoat the lid and box with Winter Blue + sealer. Apply a second coat for good coverage.

3 Sideload a 1-inch (25mm) wash brush with French Grey Blue and float it in the corners and along the edges of the lid and box. Reload the brush and slip–slap it onto the body of the lid and box for a mottled effect.

To achieve this look, you could use tissue paper instead of rice paper.

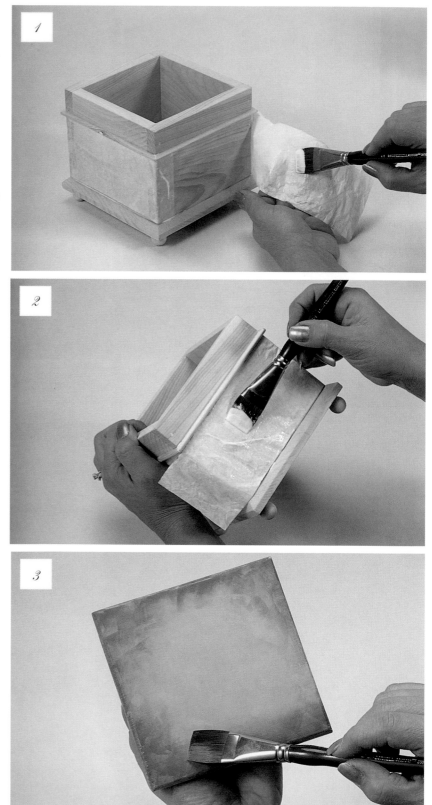

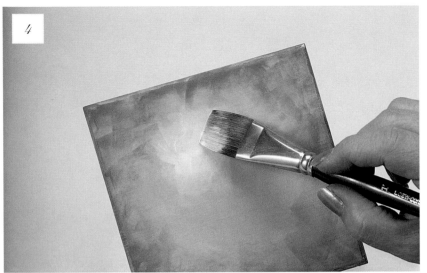

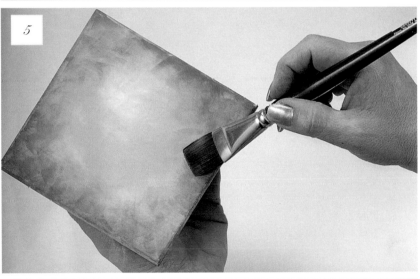

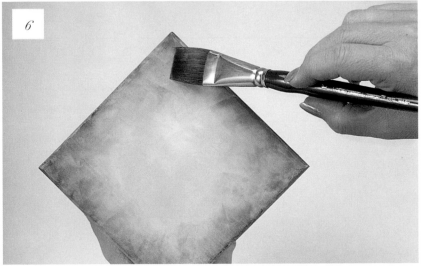

4 Sideload the brush with Blue Chiffon and slip–slap it in the center of the lid and on each side of the box.

5 Deepen each corner and the edges of the lid and box with floats of Antique Green. Use a damp no. 10 filbert to soften the floats.

6 Sideload Plantation Pine onto a ¾-inch (19mm) wash brush and float it in each corner of the lid and along the lower edge of the box. Blend the float with a damp no. 8 filbert. Complete the routed edges of the box and the legs by basecoating them with French Grey Blue, using a no. 12 shader.

7 Load a no. 12 shader with a "Medium" mix, Antique Green + Winter Blue 2:1, and base each leaf and stem.

8 Sideload the shader with a "Dark" mix, Antique Green + French Grey Blue 2:1, and walk it along the base of each leaf. Use a damp no. 8 filbert to stretch the floats. Reload the no. 12 shader with the Dark mix and make a back–to–back float, from the base of the leaf through the center, to form the shadow for the center vein line. Load a no. 6 shader with the Dark mix and float it along the right side of each stem. Sideload a no. 10 shader with a "Very Dark" mix, Plantation Pine + Antique Green + French Grey Blue + Uniform Blue 5:2:1:1, and float it within the previous Dark mix floats. Use a damp no. 8 filbert to blend the edges of the floats.

9 Sideload a "Light" mix, Jade Green + Citron Green 1:1, onto a no. 10 shader and float it in the light areas of the leaves. Reload the brush and float the Light mix along the left side of the stem. Use a damp no. 6 filbert to soften the floats. Reload the shader and use the chisel edge to pull a center vein line. Build the light areas with floats of a "Highlight" mix, Primary Yellow + Warm White 1:2. Use a damp no. 6 filbert to soften the floats.

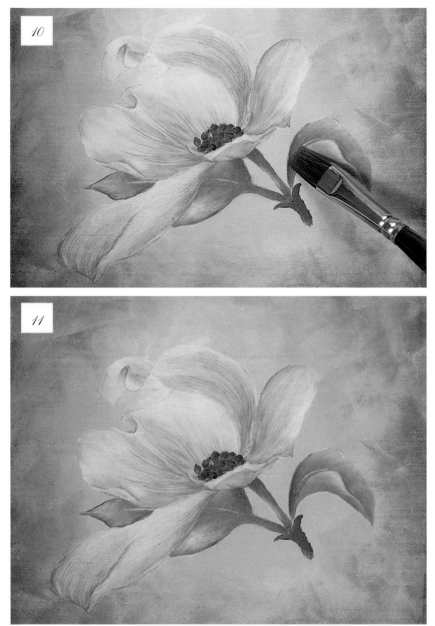

10 Sideload thinned Rookwood Red onto a no. 10 shader and add a red tint to the tip of the left leaf and along the edges of both leaves and stems.

11 Basecoat each petal with a "Medium" of French Vanilla using a no. 14 shader. Sideload thinned Moon Yellow onto a no. 14 shader, and float it through the center of Petal 1 and then float it along the right side and the bottom edge of Petal 2. This gives a warm glow to these petals.

Load a no. 14 shader with a "Dark" mix, Primary Yellow + Milk Chocolate 2:1, and walk a float at the base of Petals 1, 2 and 3. Use a damp no. 10 filbert to stretch the lines of the float. Sideload the Dark mix onto a no. 12 shader and float it under the flipped areas of Petals 2 and 4. Load a no. 4 shader with the Dark mix and float it on the back of the rolled tip of Petal 2. Reload the brush and float it on the pointed tips of Petals 2 and 4. Load a ¼-inch (6mm) filbert rake with thinned Dark mix and pull fine dark lines through the petals, following the contour. Sideload a no. 12 shader with a "Very Dark" of Winter Blue and float under each of the flipped edges on Petals 2 and 3. Load a no. 8 shader with "Very Dark" and float it along the top edge of Petal 4 and behind the fold on Petal 1. Reload the brush and float it inside the cupped area on Petal 2. Add some darker streaks using the filbert rake loaded with "Very Dark". Sideload a "2nd Very Dark" of French Grey Blue onto a no. 10 shader and float it within the previous floats to deepen them.

12 Sideload a "Light" of Buttermilk onto a no. 12 shader and walk a float in the light areas of each petal. Use a damp no. 8 filbert to stretch the lines of the float. Load the filbert rake with thinned "Light" and pull some light streaks through the petals. Build up the previously floated light areas with a float of "Highlight", Light Buttermilk. Then, sideload a "2nd Highlight," Warm White, onto a no. 8 shader and build up the highlight areas.

13 Sideload thinned Burnt Sienna onto a no. 12 shader and float orange tints on the tips of the petals and some of the edges. Use a damp no. 10 filbert to soften the floats. Deepen each float further with thinned Burnt Sienna + Cranberry Wine 1:1.

14 Base the center of the dogwood blossom with a "Medium" of Antique Green using a no. 4 shader. Use the tip of a no. 3 round brush to make tiny round dots with Citron Green. Sideload a "Dark" of Plantation Pine onto a no. 2 shader and float it around each of the dots. Use the tip of a no. 10/0 liner loaded with a "Highlight" of Primary Yellow to add a lighter area within each dot.

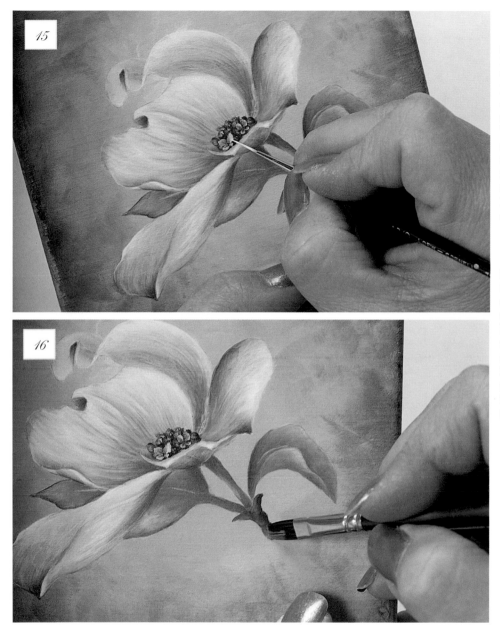

15 Use a no. 1 liner to basecoat each stamen floweret with a "Medium" of Moon Yellow. Sideload a no. 4 shader with a "Dark" mix, Milk Chocolate + Burnt Sienna 1:1, and float it at the base of each petal. Load a no. 10/0 liner with thinned "Light" mix, Primary Yellow + Warm White 1:1, and add a light edge to each petal. Add a dot of Antique Green to the center of each floweret. Add a few dots of "Medium" at the back of the center. Load a no. 10/0 liner with the Dark mix and add a tint to the top of each of these dots.

16 Use a no. 4 shader and basecoat the branch with a "Medium" of Milk Chocolate. Sideload a no. 4 shader with a "Dark" of Burnt Sienna and float it along the right side of the stem. Sideload "Very Dark", Plantation Pine, and deepen the float a bit. Sideload a "Light" mix, Primary Yellow + Milk Chocolate 2:1, on a no. 4 shader and float it along the left side of the branch and at the tips of the branch where it connects to the stem.

17 Load a no. 10 sable bright with Yellow Glaze (see page 17) and apply it to the leaves, stem and branch. Load a no. 10 sable bright with plain glazing medium and apply a thin layer to the dogwood petals.

Sideload a small amount of Olive Green onto a no. 10 sable bright and place it at the base of each leaf. Place a small amount of Olive Green at both ends of the stem and blend. Load a small amount of Charcoal Grey onto a no. 6 sable flat and deepen the shadows on each petal and on the right side of the branch. Blend with a no. 6 sable filbert. Sideload Olive Green + Charcoal Grey onto a no. 4 sable flat and place it along the bottom edge and the right side of the flower center. Use a no. 4 sable filbert to blend.

18 Sideload a clean no. 6 sable flat with Warm White mix (see page 16) and place a small amount of it in the lightest area of each petal, leaf and the stem. Use a no. 6 filbert to blend.

19 Use a no. 6 sable flat to add tints of Alizarin Crimson + Indian Yellow to the tips of Petals 2 and 4.

Add additional tints with Alizarin Crimson + Indian Yellow to the edges of Petals 2, 3 and 4 and at the base of Petal 2.

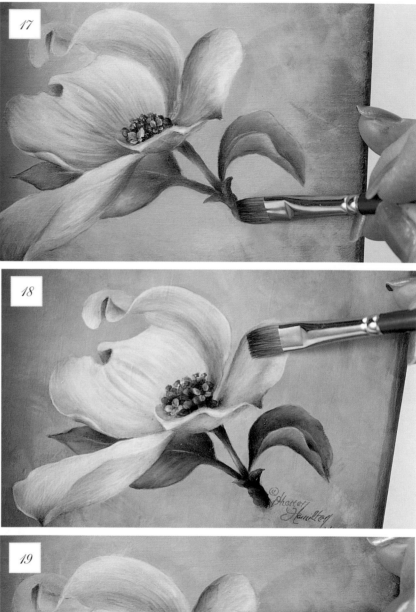

SUNFLOWER TRAY

Ahhh... the majestic sunflower bobs its head above the other flowers in the garden! I keep my feeders filled with sunflower seeds and, when the weather gets warm enough, the seeds that have fallen to the ground plant themselves and grow into these beautiful giant flowers. What a great way to keep your garden full all summer long! And when the flowers fade, a variety of birds come to feast on the left-over seeds.

Sunflowers have very interesting textures not only on the leaves, but also on the stems and petals. The petals are detailed with deep ridges and the stems are covered with fuzz. I chose to paint a wonderful woolly caterpillar and a sweet little ladybug with this project. It's so much fun to include nature's living beings along with my flowers.

This lesson will teach you how to prepare a stained and antiqued background surface for your painting. Using a stained background is a bit more difficult than using a painted background because it is harder to clean up edges of the painted elements at the end of the painting session.

PATTERN

This pattern may be hand-traced or photo-copied for personal use only. Enlarge at 175% to bring it up to full size

COLORS & MATERIALS

Antique Green
(DA)

Black Plum
(DA)

Burnt Sienna
(DA)

Citron Green
(DA)

Cranberry Wine
(DA)

Dark Chocolate
(DA)

Georgia Clay
(DA)

Jack-O-Lantern
Orange
(DA)

Lemon Yellow
(DA)

Light
Cinnamon
(DA)

Limeade
(DA)

Marigold
(DA)

Napa Red
(DA)

Pineapple
(DA)

Plantation Pine
(DA)

Primary Yellow
(DA)

Rookwood Red
(DA)

Raw Sienna
(DA)

Soft Black
(DA)

Yellow Light
(DA)

Warm White
(DA)

Cadmium
Yellow Pale
(WN)

Charcoal Grey
(WN)

Olive Green
(WN)

Purple Madder
Alizarin
(WN)

Titanium White
(WN)

Warm White
mix(WN)
(*See* page 16)

SURFACE

Large Sunflower Tray from
Wood-Ware, Inc. (*See*
Resource section)

PAINTS

DA = DecoArt
Americana Acrylics
WN = Winsor & Newton
Artists Oils

BRUSHES: LOEW-CORNELL

Comfort Series 3550
Glaze/Wash 1/2-inch
(12mm), 3/4-inch (19mm),
1-inch (25mm). Comfort
Series 3600 Oval Wash
1/2-inch (12mm). Comfort
Series 3300 Shader nos. 4, 6,
8, 10, 12, 14. Comfort Series
3500 Filbert no. 8, 10.
Comfort Series 3370 Mid
Length Liner no. 10/0.
Comfort Series 3000 Round
nos. 1, 3, 5. Comfort Filbert
Rake Series 3520 1/4-inch
(6mm). Arttec Red Sable
Series 124 Flat no. 6. Arttec
Red Sable Series 128 Filbert
nos. 4, 6. Arttec Red Sable
Series 130B Bright no. 8, 10.

ADDITIONAL SUPPLIES

Winsor & Newton Blending
& Glazing Medium. DecoArt
Gel Stain Walnut. DecoArt
Gel Stain Clear. Soft paper
towels.

1 Mix Raw Sienna + Clear Gel Stain 1:1 and apply a coat of it to the back of the tray with a 1-inch (25mm) wash brush. Use a soft paper towel and rub off the excess. When the back is dry, apply a coat of stain to the front of the tray and border trim. It may be necessary to use a stiff brush around the resin sunflowers for good coverage. Remove the excess with a paper towel. When the stain is dry, load a ³/₄-inch (19mm) wash brush with Walnut Gel Stain and apply it to the trim and in the four corners of the tray section to antique them. Use a paper towel to rub off the excess stain in the direction of the wood grain. When dry, transfer the pattern with white graphite paper.

2 Load a ³/₄-inch (19mm) wash brush with a "Medium" mix of Antique Green + Raw Sienna 2:1 and base each of the leaves. Load a no. 5 round and base the stems and calyx.

Sideload a ³/₄-inch (19mm) wash brush with a "Dark" mix of Antique Green + Plantation Pine + Burnt Sienna 2:2:1 and float it along each side of the leaf. Begin approximately one-third of the way up the leaf and float it toward the base. Use a damp ¹/₂-inch (12mm) filbert to blend the soft edge of the float. Reload the flat brush and pull a back-to-back float through the center of each leaf; use the damp filbert to blend. Load a no. 12 shader and float the "Dark" mix under the flipped areas of each leaf and around the bug hole on the large leaf. Sideload a no. 8 shader with the "Dark" mix and float it along the left side of each stem. Deepen all of the floats on the leaves and stems with floats of a "Very Dark" mix of Plantation Pine + Antique Green + Rookwood Red 4:2:1.

3 Sideload thinned Rookwood Red onto a ³/₄-inch (19mm) wash brush and float tints around the bug holes and edges of the leaves, stems and calyx. Use a ¹/₂-inch (12mm) damp oval to blend the floats. Add brighter tints of thinned Napa Red with a ¹/₂-inch (12mm) wash brush.

Repeat steps 2 and 3 on the calyx.

4 Use a ³/₄-inch (19mm) wash brush sideloaded with a "Light" mix of Antique Green + Citron Green 1:2 and float it in the center of each side of the large folded leaf at the top left of the design. Use a ¹/₂-inch (12mm) damp oval to blend. Load a ¹/₂-inch (12mm) wash brush with the "Light" mix and float it along the left and right edges of all the leaves. Use a damp no. 10 filbert to blend the float. Reload the brush and use the chisel edge of the brush to pull a vein line through the center of each leaf. Use a damp filbert to "set" the vein. Sideload the "Light" mix onto a no. 14 shader and float it on each light area of the leaves. Use a damp filbert to pull the edges of the float toward the outer leaf edge and toward the leaf center. Load a no. 12 shader brush with the "Light" mix and float it along the edge of each of the flipped areas of the leaves and the edges of the calyx. Reload the brush and use the chisel edge to pull side veins. Reload the brush again and float it along the right side of each stem.

Sideload a "Highlight" mix of Antique Green + Citron Green 1:1 onto a ¹/₂-inch (12mm) wash brush and repeat the process within the "Light" floats. Use a no. 12 shader loaded with a "2nd Highlight" of Limeade and repeat the floats.

5 Sideload a no. 8 shader with thinned "Dark" mix and float it above and below each of the side veins. Deepen the underside of each vein with a float of the "Very Dark" mix. Load a no. 10/0 liner with thinned "Dark" mix and pull very fine hairs along the stem, mostly to the left. Load the liner with thinned "Light" mix and pull some hairs throughout the stem but mostly on the right side.

6 Load a no. 5 round with a "Medium" mix of Primary Yellow + Marigold 1:1 and base each of the sunflower petals. Sideload a no. 12 shader with a "Dark," Georgia Clay, and walk a float at the base of each petal. Use a damp no. 8 filbert to stretch the lines created by the float. Sideload a no. 10 shader with "Dark" and float it under the flipped petals and on the tips of the lower flower petals. Repeat the floats with a "Very Dark," Burnt Sienna.

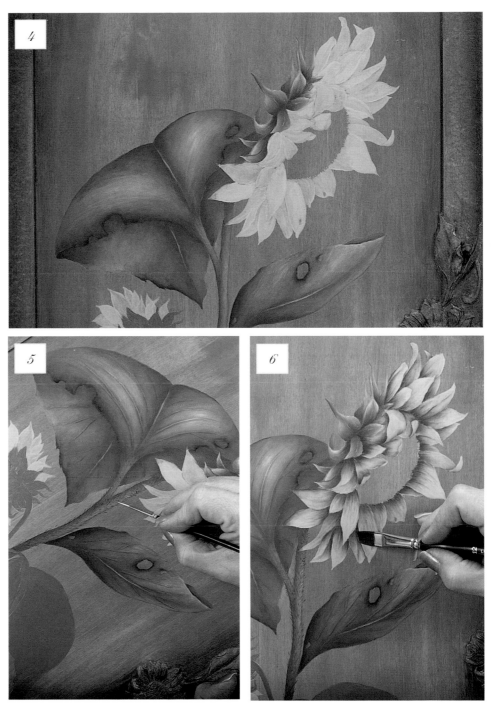

Sideload a no. 8 shader with a "2nd Very Dark," Rookwood Red, and walk a float within the "Very Dark" areas. Complete the "Dark" areas with a walked float of a "3rd Very Dark" mix of Rookwood Red + Black Plum within the already established "2nd Very Dark" areas, only on the left side of the large top sunflower and at the base of all the lower flower petals.

7 Sideload the "Light," Lemon Yellow, onto a no. 10 shader and walk a back-to-back float in the center of each petal. Use a damp no. 8 filbert to pull both ends of the float. Reload the shader and float the edges of the flipped petals. Use the chisel edge of the brush to add crisp edges to some of the petals. Sideload a no. 8 shader with the "Highlight" mix and walk a float within the established Light areas. Load a no. 10/0 liner with thinned "Highlight" mix and brighten the crisp edges. Sideload the "2nd Highlight," Pineapple, and walk a float within the 2nd Highlight areas. Finally, sideload the "3rd Highlight," Warm White mix, and walk a float only on the petals of the top flower.

8 Sideload thinned Rookwood Red onto a no. 6 shader and float it along the edges of the bug-eaten areas. Brighten the red tint with a float of thinned Napa Red.

9 For the center, load a ¼-inch (6mm) filbert rake with thinned "Dark," Dark Chocolate, and pull short, fine hairs following the contour of the flower center, pulling from the bottom upward. Don't completely cover the background; let some of it show through. Add darker hairs with a thinned "Very Dark" of Soft Black. Sideload the "Very Dark" onto a no. 12 shader and float it at the base and along both sides of the center.

10 Load the rake with thinned "Medium," Light Cinnamon, and pull lighter hairs throughout the center following the contour. Randomly add lighter hairs first with the "Light," Raw Sienna, and then with the "Highlight" mix of Pineapple + Primary Yellow 2:1.

11 Base the ladybug with a no. 3 round brush loaded with the "Medium" color, Georgia Clay.

12 Sideload the "Dark," Napa Red, onto a no. 4 shader and float it around the left side of the ladybug. Reload the brush and make a back-to-back float through the center of the bug to separate the wings.

13 Sideload the "Light" color, Jack-O-Lantern, onto a no. 4 shader and float it within the center section of each wing. Brighten the float further with Lemon Yellow.

14 Load a no. 10/0 liner with thinned soft Black and add black dots to the wings. Add the head, legs and antennae with soft Black. Complete the ladybug with an additional highlight on the wings with a float of thinned 2nd Highlight.

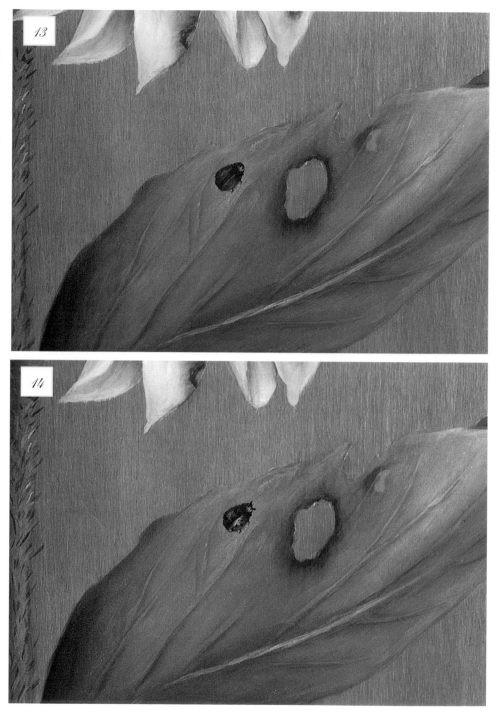

15 Load a ¼-inch (6mm) filbert rake with thinned Light Cinnamon and pull the hairs that make up the mid-section of the caterpillar. Turn your work toward you to make it easier to pull these strokes. Load the rake with thinned Dark Chocolate and base the darker front and back sections of the caterpillar.

16 Reload the rake with Dark Chocolate and pull some darker hairs in the mid-section area, mostly around the outer edges. Add some darker hairs with thinned Soft Black.

17 Load the filbert rake with thinned Raw Sienna + Primary Yellow 1:1 and add some highlights to the mid-section. Add lighter highlights with a no 10/0 liner loaded with thinned Pineapple + Raw Sienna 2:1.

Load the filbert rake with thinned Soft Black and pull some dark hairs within both end sections of the caterpillar. Add highlights with thinned Raw Sienna + Pineapple 1:1. Pull some extra hairs throughout the caterpillar with a no. 10/0 liner loaded with thinned Soft Black.

18 Apply a thin layer of yellow glaze (see page 17) to the petals, flower center, leaves, stems and calyx with a no. 8 sable bright. Deepen the darkest areas of the petals with a small amount of Purple Madder Alizarin loaded on a no. 6 sable flat. Deepen the darkest areas of the flower center with Charcoal Grey using a no. 8 sable bright. Load a no. 10 sable bright with Olive Green to deepen the leaves, stems and calyx. Use a no. 6 sable filbert to blend.

19 Sideload a no. 10 sable bright with Warm White mix and build up the highlights on the leaves. Use a no. 6 sable flat for the petals, calyx and stems and blend with a no. 6 sable filbert. Use a no. 1 round to place an additional highlight on the ladybug wings. Also, add a little highlight to the caterpillar and the center of the sunflower.

20 Sideload a very small amount of Purple Madder Alizarin onto a no. 8 sable bright and deepen the tints that have been established. Use a no. 6 sable filbert to blend.

21 Sideload Charcoal Grey onto a no. 6 sable flat and place a small amount under and to the left of the caterpillar and ladybug to create cast shadows. Use a no. 4 sable filbert to softly blend the outer edge of the paint.

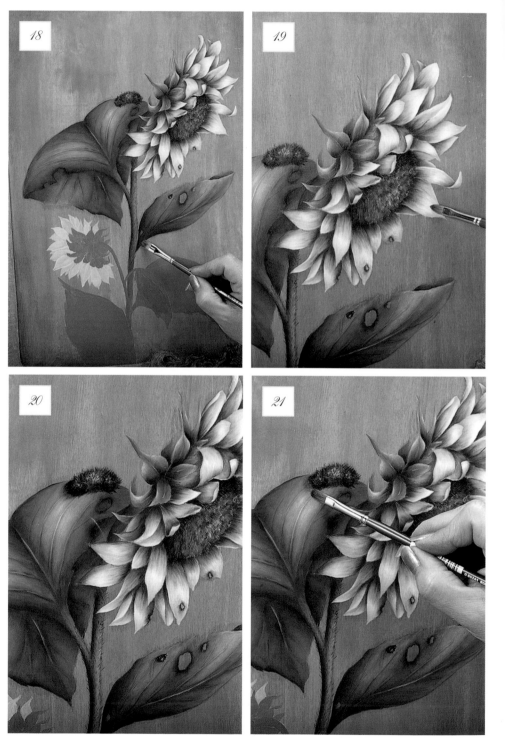

FUCHSIA HEART BOX

While I was wandering through a friend's garden, I noticed this lovely hanging fuchsia. I was inspired by the delicate yet dramatic color of the flower, and the way the light was striking the petals and buds.

From my photo, I developed my painting using a combination of warm and cool leaves, so the flower and buds would remain the focus of the design. The cool (blue-toned) leaves fade into the background while the warm (yellow-green) leaves surround the flower and lend support to it. I slip-slapped some warm green values into the background so the warm leaves wouldn't become too commanding. The cool, pink tones from the background and leaf tints help to carry the red-violet tones throughout the painting. I pulled it all together with the silver leafing on the edge.

PATTERN

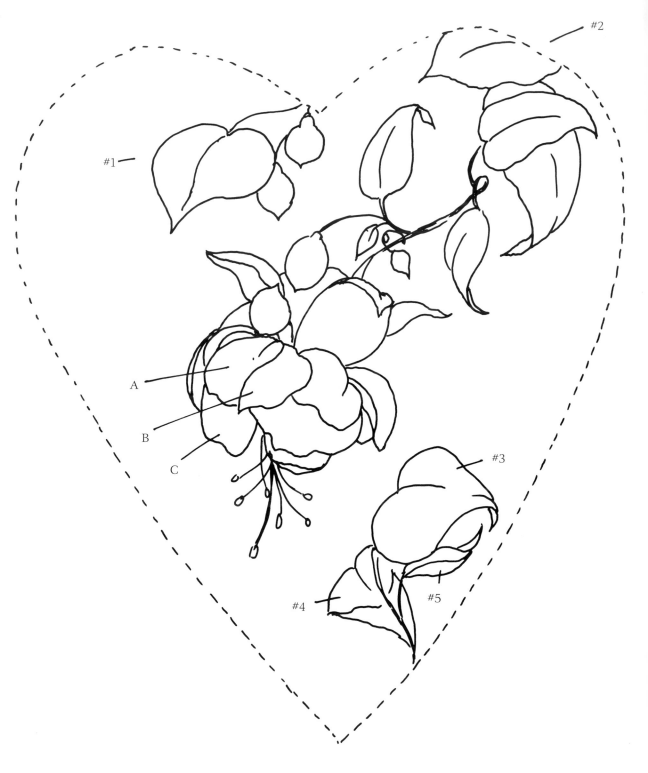

COLORS & MATERIALS

Blue Chiffon (DA)	Celery Green (DA)	Cool White (DA)	Cranberry Wine (DA)	Jade Green (DA)
Light French Blue (DA)	Lilac (DA)	Limeade (DA)	Napa Red (DA)	Payne's Grey (DA)
Royal Purple (DA)	Vivid Violet (DA)	Warm White (DA)	Winter Blue (DA)	Shimmering Silver (DM)
Cadmium Yellow Pale (WN)	Indian Yellow (WN)	Olive Green (WN)	Payne's Grey (WN)	Purple Madder Alizarin (WN)
Titanium White (WN)	Warm White mix (WN) (*See* page 16)			

SURFACE

9-inch Punched-tin heart-shaped box from Painter's Paradise (*See* Resource section)

PAINTS

DA = DecoArt Americana Acrylics
DM = DecoArt Dazzling Metallics
WN = Winsor & Newton Artists Oils

BRUSHES: LOEW-CORNELL

Comfort Series 3550 Glaze/Wash 3/4-inch (19mm), 1-inch (25mm). Comfort Series 3300 Shader nos. 2, 4, 6, 8, 10, 12, 14. Comfort Series 3500 Filbert nos. 6, 8, 10. Comfort Series 3520 Filbert Rake 1/4-inch (6mm). Comfort Series 3370 Mid Length Liner nos. 10/0, 1. Arttec Red Sable Series 124 Flat nos. 6. Arttec Red Sable Series 128 Filbert no. 6. Arttec Red Sable Series 130B Bright no. 8. Arttec Red Sable Series 120 Round no. 1. No. 12 shader.

ADDITIONAL SUPPLIES

Winsor & Newton Blending & Glazing Medium. DecoArt Multi-Purpose Sealer. Krylon Silver Leafing Pen. Magic Metallic Green Patina, Matte Interior Sealer. Krylon Matte Finish No. 1311 and Satin Varnish 7002.

1 Make a mix of Winter Blue + sealer 1:1. Basecoat the lid with a 1-inch (25mm) wash brush; apply a second coat. When the surface is dry, transfer the pattern with graphite paper. Basecoat the leaves with "Medium" mix, Winter Blue + Celery Green 3:1, using a no. 14 shader.

2 Sideload Lilac onto a 1-inch (25mm) wash brush and slip-slap it onto the left center side of the lid for a mottled background. Next, sideload Napa Red + Winter Blue 1:1; slip-slap it within the wet Lilac area. Sideload Celery Green and slip-slap it into the upper-right corner, extending it across the top of the heart a bit. Reload the brush and slip-slap it into the right corner again, working it downward along the right side of the heart. Use a no. 10 damp filbert to soften and blend.

3 Sideload a "Dark" mix, Medium mix + Light French Blue 5:2, onto a no. 14 shader and float it along the side and across the base of each leaf. Use a damp no. 10 filbert to blend the float. Reload the brush and make a back–to–back float down the center of the leaf, beginning the float at the base. Use a damp no. 8 filbert to stretch the edge of the float toward the leaf edge. Sideload the Dark mix onto a no. 10 shader and float it on the tip of some of the leaves. Sideload the Dark mix onto a no. 4 shader and float it at the base and along the right side of each of the stems attached to the light leaf. Deepen the established dark floats at the base and through the center of the leaves and at the base of the stems with floats of "Very Dark" mix, Celery Green + Light French Blue 1:2 + Payne's Grey 1½:1.

4 Sideload a "Light" mix, Blue Chiffon + Celery Green 3:1, onto a no. 10 shader. Make a back–to–back float in the light area and float it along the edge of each leaf. Use a damp no. 8 filbert to stretch the float, pulling the brush at an angle toward the edge or toward the center vein area. Reload the shader and use the chisel edge to pull the center vein line. With a no. 8 shader, repeat all of the floats with "Highlight" mix, Limeade + Cool White 1:1. Blend with a damp no. 6 filbert. Reload the shader and use the chisel edge to build up the highlight in the center vein line. Sideload the brush with a "2nd Highlight," Warm White, and brighten all the highlight areas. Add an additional highlight to the vein line with "2nd Highlight". Repeat this process with the stems.

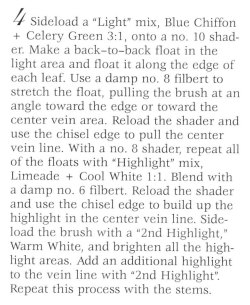

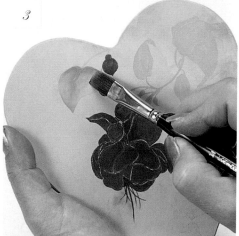

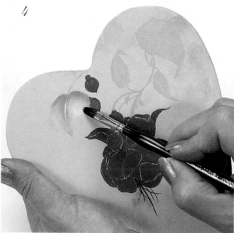

When you pull a center vein line, be sure to begin away from the back edge of the leaf and lift up on the brush pressure before reaching the tip. It also helps to use a damp filbert to stretch both ends of the vein line to "set" it in.

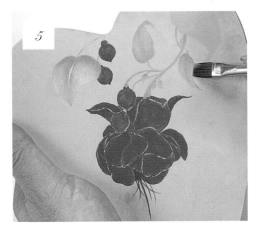

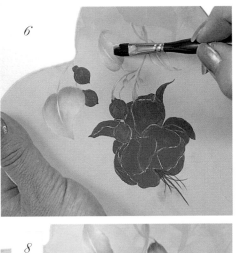

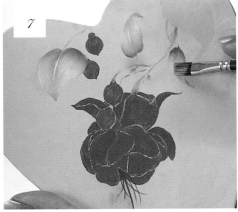

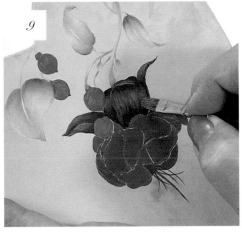

5 Base the leaves with a "Medium" mix of Celery Green + Winter Blue 1:1, using a no. 14 shader. Sideload the shader with a "Dark" mix of Celery Green + Light French Blue 1:2, and float it along the back edge of the leaves. Then make a back–to–back float with the Dark mix through the center to establish the shadow for the vein line. Float the Dark mix at the beginning and end of each stem. On the small leaves, float the Dark mix around the back edges. Using a no. 10 shader, float "Very Dark" mix floats of Dark mix + Payne's Grey 1½:1, within the established dark floats.

6 Sideload a no. 10 shader with "Light" mix, Jade Green + Blue Chiffon 1:2, and float it along the leaf edges. Reload the brush and pull the center vein line with the chisel edge. Use a no. 6 damp filbert to blend the floats. Float the Light mix along the top or left sides of the leaves. Float the Light mix on the tips of the small leaves. Repeat these floats with the "Highlight" mix, Limeade + Cool White 1:1. Blend the floats with a damp no. 6 filbert. Load a no. 8 shader with the "2nd Highlight," Warm White, and brighten the highlights further.

7 Load thinned Cranberry Wine onto a no. 12 shader and float tints in the dark area of some leaves and stems. Use the lower petal's "Highlight" mix, Cool White + Vivid Violet + Napa Red 4:1:1, and add tints of thinned lower petal's "Medium" mix, Cranberry Wine + Vivid Violet + Winter Blue 5:1:1, in the light–to medium–value areas of some leaves.

8 Base the petals with the "Medium" mix, Cranberry Wine + Winter Blue + Vivid Violet + Royal Purple 5:1:1:1, using a no. 10 shader. Sideload a "Dark" of Cranberry Wine onto it and walk a float at the base of the petals. Stretch the edges of the float to get a jagged, veinlike effect. Reload the brush and float "Dark" under the flipped area and between the petals to separate them. Load a no. 8 shader with a "Very Dark" of Royal Purple and repeat the floats within the previous floats. Float the "2nd Very Dark" mix, Royal Purple + Payne's Grey 1:1, and repeat the floats on some areas to deepen the values further.

9 Sideload the "Light" mix, Blue Chiffon + Vivid Violet + Cranberry Wine 4:1:1, onto a no. 8 shader and walk a back-to-back float through the largest petal's center. Use a damp no. 6 filbert to stretch the edges of the float. Float a bit on the left edge of the petal, on the petal at the extreme left, and on the tip of the flipped petal. Load a ¼-inch (6mm) filbert rake with thinned Light mix and pull fine lines onto each petal following the contour.

When blending with the filbert, be sure to blend in the direction of the side leaf veins. When blending a flower petal you must blend in the direction of the petal contour.

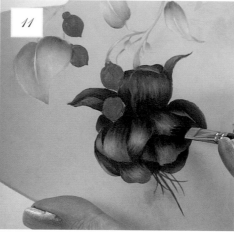

10 Base each petal with the "Medium" mix, Cranberry Wine + Vivid Violet + Winter Blue 5:1:1, using a no. 12 shader. Sideload a "Dark" of Cranberry Wine onto a no. 12 shader and walk a float at the base of each petal. Use the chisel edge of a no. 8 filbert to stretch the floats. Sideload a no. 10 shader with the "Very Dark" mix, Royal Purple + Payne's Grey 4:1, to deepen all of the previous floats.

11 Sideload "Light" mix, Vivid Violet + Winter Blue 3:1, onto a no. 8 shader. Make a back–to–back float through the center of Petals A, B and C; use a damp no. 6 filbert to stretch both ends of the float. Reload and float it along the left and lower edges of the remaining petals. Use a damp no. 6 filbert to stretch the ends of the floats. Load a ¼–inch (6mm) filbert rake with thinned Light mix and pull very fine lines through each petal, following the petal contour. Sideload the "Highlight" mix, Cool White + Vivid Violet + Napa Red 4:1:1, onto a no. 8 shader and float it within the previous light floats; use a damp no. 6 filbert to stretch the floats. Pull fine lines with the filbert rake loaded with the Highlight mix. Build the highlights further, loading Cool White onto the filbert rake and pulling very fine lines through the highlights of the lightest petals.

12 Using a no. 8 shader, apply tints of thinned Napa Red to the top petals and thinned Vivid Violet to the lower petals.

13 Base the buds with a no. 8 shader with a "Medium" mix, Winter Blue + Vivid Violet + Cranberry Wine 1:1:5. Sideload Royal Purple onto a no. 8 shader and float it along the right side of each bud. Make a narrower float of Royal Purple along the left side. Load a ¼–inch (6mm) filbert rake with thinned Royal Purple and pull some fine lines through the buds following the contour. Deepen the right side of each bud with a float of "Very Dark" mix, Cranberry Wine + Payne's Grey 4:1, on a no. 6 shader. Sideload a no. 6 shader with the "Warm Leaves Dark" mix, Celery Green + Light French Blue 1:2, and add a green tint along the bottom of each bud.

When floating darks or highlights, always paint within the previous floats. This helps to create the illusion of a rounded shape.

14 Sideload the "Light" mix, Blue Chiffon + Vivid Violet + Cranberry Wine 4:1:1, onto a no. 6 shader and make a back–to–back float in the light area of each bud. Use a damp no. 6 filbert to stretch the edges of the float to follow the contour of the bud. Load a 1/4–inch (6mm) filbert rake with thinned Light mix and pull some additional fine lines through the light area. Build each of the light areas up with a float of "Highlight", Cool White, using a no. 4 shader.

15 Load a no. 1 liner with thinned "Medium" mix, Napa Red + Winter Blue 1:1, and pull the pistil and stamens. Add three dots at the end of the pistil with the liner loaded with the Medium mix. Sideload the "Dark" mix, Winter Blue + Vivid Violet + Cranberry Wine 1:1:5, onto a no. 2 shader and place the Dark mix at both ends of the pistil and stamens. Float the Dark mix along the bottom edge and at the ends of the stamen. Float the Dark mix along the left side of the dots at the end of the pistil. Load a no. 10/0 liner with a "Very Dark" of Royal Purple and deepen both ends of the pistil.

16 Load a no. 10/0 liner with thinned Light mix and place a dot on the left side of each of the pistil ends. Add the Light mix to the center of each stamen and pistil. Load a no. 10/0 liner with thinned Warm White and pull lighter lines within the previous ones.

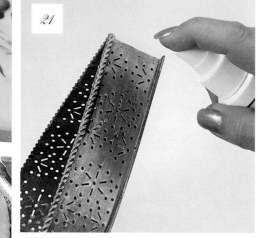

17 Apply Yellow Glaze (see page 17) to the buds and top fuchsia petals with a no. 8 sable bright. Apply the plain glazing medium to the lower petals and leaves. Sideload Purple Madder Alizarin onto a no. 6 sable flat and deepen the dark areas of the buds and petals. Use a no. 6 sable filbert to blend. Deepen the lower petals further with Payne's Grey. Use a no. 6 sable filbert to blend. Deepen the upper petals and buds further with Purple Madder Alizarin + Payne's Grey. For the leaves, deepen with Payne's Grey + Olive Green and blend with a no. 6 sable filbert.

18 Sideload Warm White mix (see page 16) onto a no. 6 sable flat and build up the highlights on the petals, buds, leaves and stems. Use a clean no. 6 sable filbert to blend. Load a no. 1 round with Warm White mix thinned with glazing medium and build up the highlights on the stems and pistil.

19 Add Purple Madder Alizarin tints to the leaves and stems using a no. 6 sable flat. Blend with a no. 6 sable filbert.

20 Apply the silver leafing after the varnish has been sprayed on the lid. Varnish dulls the leafing, so it is important to apply it only after the varnishing has been completed. Shake the pen very well. Remove the cap and push the tip down gently onto a waxed palette to load the tip of the pen. Carefully pull the pen across the edge of the lid to deposit the silver paint.

21 Paint the sides of the box with Shimmering Silver using a ³/₄–inch (19mm) wash brush. When dry, spray the surface with Magic Metallic Green Patina. Allow time for the patina to dry and oxidize and then apply a coat of Matte Interior Sealer to seal the surface.

MORNING GLORY BIRDHOUSE

Each year, morning glory vines are entwined around the fences and posts that hold my birdfeeders. I'm fascinated that these beautiful blossoms seem to wake up each morning and quietly fall asleep when the sun goes down. I thought it very appropriate to paint these sweet flowers wrapped around this tiny birdhouse.

Morning glories are cone-shaped flowers with deep throats, made up of a single, continuous petal. In the lesson, you will learn to develop their shape using various values to separate the front plane of the flower from the back plane. You will also learn to create the delicate, rippled edges by using a series of walked floats.

I used a combination of metal paints with a blue patina to paint the roof, base and perch in order to pull the cool blue-green colors from the leaves throughout the project. Unusual treatments like this can enhance the overall project and add to its appeal.

This pattern
may be
hand-traced
or photo-
copied for
personal
use only.
Enlarge at
125% to
bring it up
to full size.

COLORS & MATERIALS

Admiral Blue
(DA)

Arbor Green
(DA)

Blue Chiffon
(DA)

Blue Violet
(DA)

Indian
Turquoise
(DA)

Light
Buttermilk
(DA)

Red Iron Oxide
(DA)

Royal Purple
(DA)

Sapphire
(DA)

Taffy Cream
(DA)

Winter Blue
(DA)

Wisteria
(DA)

Cadmium
Yellow Pale
(WN)

Indian Yellow
(WN)

Olive Green
(WN)

Payne's Grey
(WN)

Purple Madder
Alizarin
(WN)

Titanium White
(WN)

Warm White
mix (WN)
(*See* page 16)

SURFACE

Round birdhouse from Michael's

BRUSHES: LOEW-CORNELL

Comfort Series 3550 Glaze/Wash 3/4-inch (19mm), 1–inch (25mm). Comfort Series 3300 Shader nos. 2, 6, 8, 10, 12, 14. Comfort Series 3500 Filbert nos. 6, 8. Comfort Series 3050 Script Liner no. 2. Comfort Series 3370 Mid Length Liner nos. 10/0, 1. Arttec Red Sable Series 124 Flat no. 6. Arttec Red Sable Series 130B Bright nos. 8, 10. Arttec Red Sable Series 128 Filbert no. 6.

ADDITIONAL SUPPLIES

Winsor & Newton Blending & Glazing Medium. DecoArt Multi-Purpose Sealer. Magic Metallic Copper and Dark Bronze Metallics. Aqua Blue Patina. Matte Interior Sealer. Sandpaper.

1 Sand all the surfaces of the birdhouse and then remove the dust. Use a ³/₄-inch (19mm) wash brush to basecoat the roof, perch and base with Red Iron Oxide + sealer 1:1. When dry, apply two coats of Copper Metallic + Dark Bronze Metallic 2:1. Use a 1-inch (25mm) wash brush to basecoat the body of the birdhouse with two coats of Winter Blue + sealer 1:1. Sand between the coats to smooth the surface. Apply the pattern with white graphite paper.

2 Load a ³/₄-inch (19mm) wash brush with the Aqua Blue Patina. While the second coat of metallic paint is still wet, apply the patina with a ³/₄-inch (19mm) wash brush. It will appear clear as you apply it, but it will oxidize and the blue patina color will show in about a half hour. In this shot, you see the patina being applied at the bottom of the birdhouse. The process is half completed on the roof to the left and the finished product is on the right.

3 Seal the surface with Matte Interior Sealer using a ³/₄-inch (19mm) wash brush.

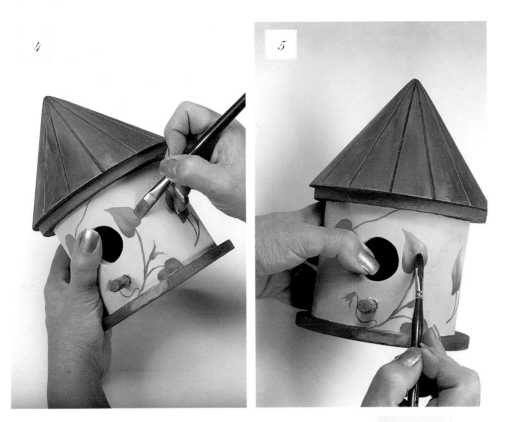

4 Load a no. 14 shader with the "Medium" Leaf mix, Arbor Green + Indian Turquoise + Blue Violet + Wisteria 4:2:1:2, and basecoat the leaves and stems. Sideload the "Dark" mix, Arbor Green + Indian Turquoise + Blue Violet 2:1:1, onto a no. 12 shader and float it at the base of each leaf. Reload the brush and pull a back-to-back float through the center of each leaf to develop the shadow for the center vein line. Sideload a no. 8 shader with the " leaf mix and float it at the base and along the left side of each stem. Sideload the "Very Dark" leaf mix, Arbor Green + Blue Violet 1:2, onto a no. 10 shader and float it within the previous dark floats.

5 Sideload the "Light" leaf mix, Indian Turquoise + Blue Chiffon + Arbor Green 2:2:1, onto a no. 12 shader and walk a float along the light edges of the leaves. Then take a damp no. 8 filbert and soften the blend. Reload the shader with the Light mix and use the chisel edge to place the center vein line. Float the Light mix along the right side of each stem and along the top edge of the calyx. Blend, using the flat edge of the filbert.

6 Load a no. 10 shader with the "Highlight" mix, Blue Chiffon + Indian Turquoise + Arbor Green 3:1:1, and build up the highlights within the previous Light mix floats. Blend the float with a no. 8 filbert. Build up the lights on the stem and calyx with the Highlight mix. Sideload a no. 8 shader with the "2nd Highlight" of Blue Chiffon and build up the highlights a bit more on all the elements. Blend with a damp no. 6 filbert.

7 Sideload thinned Wisteria onto a no. 12 shader and float light purple tints in the light areas on some leaves. Sideload thinned Blue Violet onto a no. 12 shader and float it in the base of some leaves. Add additional purple tints with thinned Royal Purple.

8 Basecoat the base of the trumpets using a no. 8 shader loaded with a "Medium" of Wisteria. Float a thinned "Dark" of Royal Purple along the left side and at the base of the trumpets.
    Sideload a no. 6 shader with a "Light" of Taffy Cream and float it under the petal edge and along the right side of the trumpet.

9 Base the petals with "Medium" using a no. 14 shader. Sideload "Light" onto a no. 12 shader and walk a float from the throat outward, following the petal contour. Use the tip of a damp no. 8 filbert to stretch the lines created by the walked float out into the body of the petal.

10 Sideload a no. 10 shader with a "Highlight" of Light Buttermilk and walk a lighter float in the throat. Use the tips of a damp no. 6 filbert to stretch the lines of the float.

11 Sideload a "Dark" of Sapphire onto a no. 12 shader and walk a float along the outer edges of the petals. Use a damp no. 8 filbert to stretch the float following the petal contour. Repeat the "Dark" float if necessary. Float "Dark" along the top-front edge of the throat.

12 Use a no. 12 shader to walk a float of "Very Dark", Blue Violet, along the edges to create tiny triangle–like areas of color. Use a damp filbert to stretch the float. Sideload a no. 10 shader and walk a float of "2nd Very Dark", Admiral Blue, within the small triangular areas. Stretch the edge of the float with a damp filbert.

13 Sideload a no. 8 shader with "Light" and pull a back-to-back float through the center of the petal. Use a damp no. 6 filbert to stretch the float. Sideload the brush with "Highlight" and repeat the process.

14 Load a no. 2 liner with Wisteria and pull stripes on each petal. Sideload a no. 2 shader with Royal Purple and float it on each inside edge of the stripe. Load a no. 10/0 liner with thinned "Highlight" and pull a few lighter lines inside the stripe.

15 Use a no. 10/0 liner with thinned "Highlight" to pull little C-stroke type stamens in the center of the throat. Load a no. 1 liner with thinned "Medium" leaves, stems and tendrils mix, Arbor Green + Indian Turquoise + Blue Violet + Wisteria 4:2:1:2, and paint the tendrils. Load a no. 10/0 liner with "Dark" leaves, stems and tendrils mix of Arbor Green + Indian Turquoise + Blue Violet 2:1:1, and place it at the beginning and ends of the tendrils and the crossing-over points. Load a no. 10/0 liner with a "Light" leaves, stems and tendrils mix of Indian Turquoise + Blue Chiffon + Arbor Green 2:2:1, and place light areas in the tendrils.

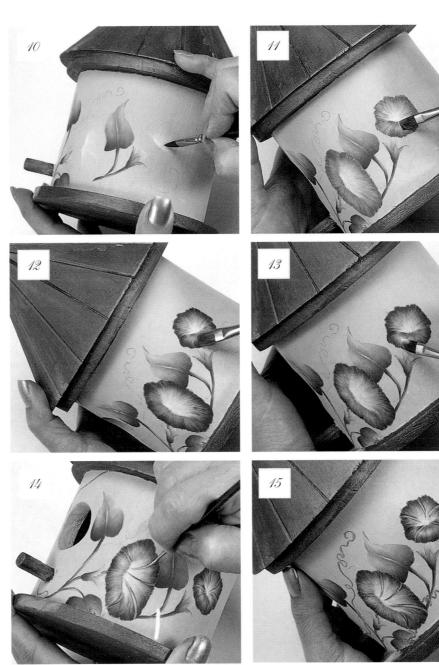

16 Apply a thin layer of glazing medium to the leaves, stems and tendrils with a no. 8 sable bright. Load a no. 8 sable bright with Olive Green + Payne's Grey and deepen the darkest areas of the leaves, stems and tendrils. Use a no. 6 sable filbert to blend.

Apply glazing medium to each flower with a no. 10 sable bright. Load a no. 10 sable bright with Payne's Grey and deepen the darkest areas of each flower. Take a no. 6 sable filbert and blend.

17 Apply Warm White mix (see page 16), to the highlight areas of the leaves, flowers, stems and tendrils with a no. 6 sable flat. Use a no. 6 sable filbert to blend.

18 Use a no. 8 sable bright with Purple Madder Alizarin to add tints to the leaves and flowers. Use a no. 6 sable filbert to blend. Load a no. 6 sable flat with Indian Yellow and add a scant amount to the top of the flower throat to accentuate the yellow tint. Use a no. 6 sable filbert to blend.

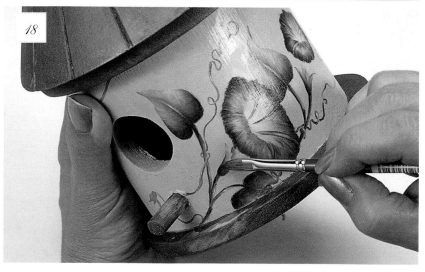

DAFFODIL &
BUTTERFLY BOX

Daffodils are one of the first flowers to bloom in the spring after a long, cold winter. Each year I can't wait to see their wonderful yellow buds pushing up out of the snow, because I know that spring is not too far away!

This lesson combines the techniques that you have learned from previous projects, such as using walked floats to create a ridged effect, to paint the outer petals and work the cone-shaped daffodil trumpet.

I sponged a bit of gold around the edges of the lid and the bottom of this sweet little heart box to add some interest and carry the yellow tones from the flower and butterfly through the painting.

© Sharon
2002 Hamilton MDA

This pattern may be hand-traced or photocopied for personal use only. Reduce to 90% before using.

COLORS & MATERIALS

Antique Green
(DA)

Buttermilk
(DA)

Charcoal Grey
(DA)

Eggshell
(DA)

French Vanilla
(DA)

Grey Sky
(DA)

Light
Buttermilk
(DA)

Marigold
(DA)

Milk Chocolate
(DA)

Moon Yellow
(DA)

Neutral Grey
(DA)

Olde Gold
(DA)

Rookwood Red
(DA)

Taffy Cream
(DA)

Titanium White
(DA)

Glorious Gold
(DM)

Alizarin
Crimson
(WN)

Cadmium
Yellow Pale
(WN)

Charcoal Grey
(WN)

Indian Yellow
(WN)

Olive Green
(WN)

Titanium White
(WN)

Warm White
mix (WN)
(*See* page 16.)

SURFACE

Wooden puffed heart-shaped box from Gretchen Cagle Publications (*See* Resource section)

PAINTS

DA = DecoArt Americana Acrylics
DM = DecoArt Dazzling Metallics
WN = Winsor & Newton Artists Oils

BRUSHES: LOEW-CORNELL

Comfort Series 3550 Glaze/Wash 3/4-inch (19mm). Comfort Series 3000 Round no. 3. Comfort Series 3300 Shader nos. 4, 6, 8, 10, 12, 14. Comfort Series 3500 Filbert nos. 6, 8, 10. Comfort Series 3520 Filbert Rake 1/4-inch (6mm). Comfort Series 3370 Mid Length Liner no. 10/0. Arttec Series 124 Flat no. 6. Arttec Series 128 Filbert no. 6. Arttec Series 130B Sable Bright no. 8.

ADDITIONAL SUPPLIES

Winsor & Newton Blending and Glazing Medium. DecoArt Multi-Purpose Sealer. Small silk sponge.

1 Load a ¾-inch (19mm) wash brush and basecoat the box with Eggshell + sealer 1:1. Apply a second coat for good coverage. Sideload the brush with Eggshell + Light Buttermilk 1:1 and float it in the upper left, the area behind the left side of the daffodil. Use a damp no.10 filbert to soften the outer edges of the float.

Sideload the ¾-inch (19mm) wash brush with Eggshell + Charcoal Grey (DA) + Neutral Grey 2:2:1 and float it around the upper and lower edges of the bottom portions of the heart box. Reload the brush and float the mix around the outer edge of the lid.

2 When the lid is dry, transfer the pattern lightly with gray graphite paper.

Dampen a small silk sponge with water and squeeze out the excess. Tap the sponge into a bit of Glorious Gold. Tap off the excess paint onto a piece of waxed palette paper then use the sponge to stipple around the outer edge of the lid and base of the box.

3 Base the leaves and stem with Charcoal Grey (DA) + Grey Sky, 2:1 using a no. 8 shader.

Basecoat the brown, papery part of the stem with Marigold + Milk Chocolate + Buttermilk 1:1:1, using a no. 6 shader.

Use a no. 14 shader to basecoat the petals with Buttermilk.

Base the body of the butterfly with Marigold + Rookwood Red 3:1, using a no. 3 round.

Base the wings with Buttermilk, using a no. 10 shader.

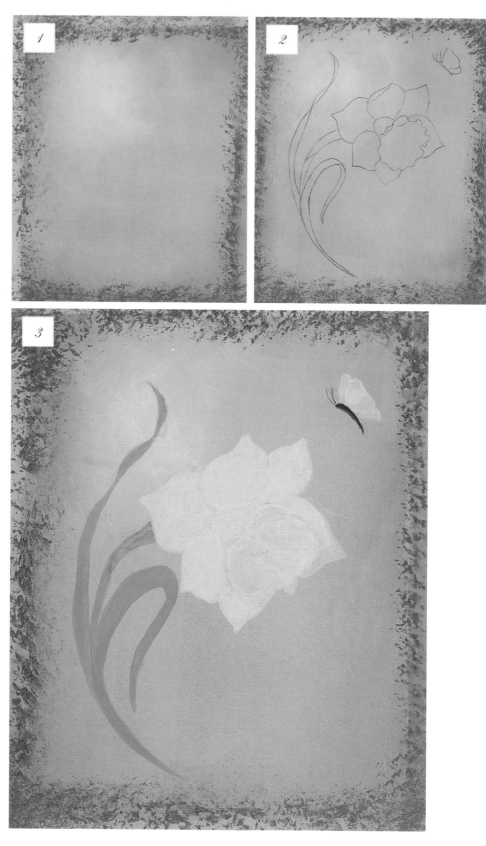

4 Sideload a no. 8 shader with Charcoal Grey (DA) + Neutral Grey + Antique Green 2:2:1, and float it at the top, base and along the left side of the stem. Use a damp no. 6 filbert to soften. Reload the shader and float along the left side of the leaves and under the turned areas.

Sideload Marigold onto a no. 6 shader and float it under the daffodil petal and along the left side of the stem.

Sideload Moon Yellow onto a no. 14 shader and walk a float at the base of each petal. Use the tips of a damp no. 8 filbert to pull the edges of the float toward the petal center. Sideload Moon Yellow onto a no. 14 shader and walk a float inside the flower's throat and around the flower cup base. Use a damp filbert to stretch the edges of the float. Sideload Marigold onto a no. 12 shader and repeat within the established Moon Yellow floats. Use a damp no. 8 filbert to stretch the floats. Sideload Olde Gold onto a no. 10 shader and walk a float in the dark areas. Sideload Charcoal Grey (DA) onto a no. 8 shader and float it in the darkest areas of the petals.

Sideload thinned Charcoal Grey (DA) onto a no. 6 shader and float it along the top edge of the butterfly.

Sideload Moon Yellow onto a no. 6 shader and walk a float between the wings to separate them. Use a damp no. 6 filbert to stretch the floats. Sideload Marigold onto a no. 4 shader and deepen the previous floats.

5 Sideload Charcoal Grey (DA) + Grey Sky + French Vanilla 1:1:1 onto a no. 6 shader and make a back-to-back float in the center of each leaf. Reload the brush and float the mix along the right edge of each leaf.

Sideload the same mix onto a no. 4 shader and float it along the right side of the stem.

Sideload Light Buttermilk onto a no. 12 shader and walk a float around the outer edges of the petals. Use a damp no. 8 filbert to stretch the edges of the floats. Reload the shader and make a back-to-back float in the center of Petals A, B, C and D and in the lightest area of the cup or trumpet. Use a damp no. 8 filbert to stretch the edges of the float.

Reload the brush with Light Buttermilk and walk a float along the top edge of the inside of the flower cup. Use a damp filbert to stretch the edges of the float.

Use a no. 10/0 liner with Marigold + Buttermilk 1:2 and pull some hairs along the bottom edge of the butterfly body.

Sideload Light Buttermilk onto a no. 6 shader and walk a float along the front tip of each wing.

6 Sideload a no. 6 shader with taffy Creamand float it within each of the previous light areas.

Load a ¼-inch (6mm) filbert rake with thinned Charcoal Grey + Grey Sky + French Vanilla 1:1:1 and pull some fine lines through this section of the stem. Load a no. 10/0 liner with thinned Taffy Cream and add some highlights within the previous lines.

Brighten the lightest areas on the right side of the flower with walked floats of Titanium White using a no. 10 shader. Use a damp no. 6 filbert to stretch the ends of the floats.

Sideload Titanium White onto a no. 4 shader and float it at the front edge and top of the wings.

Daffodil and Butterfly

7 Sideload thinned Marigold onto a no. 8 shader and add some yellow tints to the stem and leaves in the medium-value areas. Add some darker tints with Marigold + Rookwood Red 3:1 in the darker areas of the leaves.

Sideload thinned Marigold + Rookwood Red 2:1 onto a no. 10 shader and float red tints along the edges of some of the petals and inside the throat of the daffodil.

Load a no. 10/0 liner with thinned Marigold and pull five stamens in the throat of the flower. Add a dot to the end of each stamen and then shade each stamen end with Marigold + Rookwood Red 2:1. Add a highlight to each one with Marigold + Buttermilk 1:2.

Sideload thinned Charcoal Grey (DA) onto a no. 4 shader and float it only in the darkest areas of the butterfly wings.

Load a no. 10/0 liner with thinned Marigold and place a small dark dot at the front of each wing. Then pull a series of lines along the front edges and tips of the wings. Pull the lines for the antennae using a no. 10/0 liner loaded with thinned Marigold. Add dots of Marigold to the end of each antenna using the tip of the liner. Use the liner to add faint vein lines in each wing.

Add a red tint to the base of the wings with a float of thinned Marigold + Rookwood Red 2:1, using a no. 6 shader.

Oil Glazing

8 Apply plain glazing medium to the leaves, stem, petals and butterfly with a no. 6 sable flat. Sideload a bit of Olive Green onto a no. 6 sable flat and place it in the darkest area of each leaf and the stem. Use a no. 6 sable filbert to blend the paint.

Sideload a small amount of Warm White mix onto a clean no. 6 sable flat and place it in the highlight area of the stem and each leaf. Use a no. 6 sable filbert to blend the paint.

Use the glazing brush to pick up a very tiny amount of Indian Yellow and place it in the throat of the daffodil and at the base of the darker petals. Use a no. 6 sable filbert to blend.

Sideload Warm White mix onto a clean no. 8 sable bright and place it in the highlight area of each petal and the flower cup. Use a no. 6 sable filbert to blend the paint. Reload the brush and build up the highlights on the butterfly wings.

Sideload Charcoal Grey (WN) onto the no. 6 sable flat that was used for the leaf darks and place a few deeper shadows within the darkest areas of the petals and wings of the butterfly. Blend the paint with a no. 6 sable filbert.

Add some reddish tints to the petals and the throat of the daffodil with Alizarin Crimson + Indian Yellow using a clean no. 6 sable flat. Use a no. 6 sable filbert to blend.

Barb Watson's Brushworks

P.O. Box 1467
Moreno Valley, CA 92556
www.barbwatson.com
Phone 909-653-3780
Fax 909-653-5573
17" Scoop Plate (Project Five)

ColArt Americas, Inc.

11 Constitution Avenue
P.O. Box 1396
Piscataway, NJ 08855-1396
www.winsornewton.com
Phone 732-562-0770
Fax 732-562-0940
Winsor & Newton Oil Paints
& Glazing Medium

DecoArt

P.O. Box 386
Stanford, KY 40484
www.decoart.com
Phone 606-365-3193
Fax 606-365-9739
Acrylic Paints and mediums

Gretchen Cagle Publications, Inc.

P.O. Box 2104
Claremore, OK 74018
www.gretchencagle.com
Phone 918-342-1080
Fax 918-341-8909
Puffed Heart Box
(Project Ten)

Loew-Cornell, Inc.

563 Chestnut Ave.
Teaneck, NJ 07666-2491
www.loew-cornell.com
Phone 201-836-7070
Fax 201-836-8110
Brushes

Mayco Magic Metallics

4077 Weaver Court South
Hilliard, OH 43026
www.magicmetallics.com
Phone 614-876-1171

Michaels Stores, Inc.

Michaels.com
8000 Bent Branch Dr.
Irving, TX 75063
www.michaels.com
Phone 800-642-4235
Birdhouse (Project Nine)

Painters Paradise

Jo C. & Co.
C-10 950 Ridge Rd.
Claymont, DE 19703-3553
www.paintersparadise.com
Phone 302-798-3897
Fax 302-478-9441
Heart Ornaments (Project Two)
Mail Keeper (Project Four)
Spice Bin (Project Three)
Punched Tin Heart-shaped Box
(Project Eight)
Krylon Gold Leafing Pen
Krylon Silver Leafing Pen

Wood Concepts

3000 Milford Rd.
East Stroudsburg, PA 18301
www.woodconceptsstudio.com
Phone 570-424-3310
Fax 570-424-3312
Domed Clock (Project One)
Square Tea Box (Project Six)

Wood-Ware, Inc.

P.O. Box 100746
Cape Coral, FL 33910
www.wood-ware.net
Phone 866-579-3837
Fax 530-425-3218
Tray (Project Seven)

INDEX

A

Acrylic brush
    fully loading, 11
    sideloading, 12
Acrylics
    basecoating, 12-13
    labeling and setting up palette, 11
Antiquing, 22
    background, 87

B

Background
    crackling, 19, 22
    creating depth, 65
    getting oil on, 72
    out-of-focus, 75
    preparing, 48
    stained, 87
Back-to-back float, 14, 25
Basecoating, 22-23, 122
    acrylic, 12
Bee, 24, 61
Berries, 42
Birdhouse, 108-117
Blending
    with filbert, 14, 103
    oils, 42
Blossoms
    dogwood, 80-83
    wisteria, 69-71
Box
    daffodil and butterfly, 118-125
    dogwood, 74-85
    heart, 98-107
Brushes, 8
    for glazing, 38, 52. *See also* Acrylic brush
Buds
    dogwood, 80
    fuchsia, 104-105
    wisteria, 70
Butterfly, 118-125

C

Cast shadows, 51, 62
Caterpillar, 95
Chicory, 25
Clock, wood casing, 18-29
Color wash, 15
Crackle medium, 22
Crocus, 34-37
C-strokes, 115

D

Daffodil, 118-125
Daylilies, 45-53
Dogwood, 74-85

E

Edges
    cleaning up, 16
    rippled, 109

F

Faux finish, 45
Filbert, blending techniques with, 14
Filbert rake, for texture, 55, 59, 95
Fleabane, 26
Floats, 13-14
Flowers. *See also* Blossoms, Buds, Chicory, Crocus, Daylilies, Dogwood, Fleabane, Fuchsia, Morning Glory, Petals, Sunflower, Tulips, Wildflowers, Wisteria
Fuchsia, 98-107

G

Glaze, yellow, 17
Glazing. See Oil glazing
Gold leafing, 52, 62

H

Heart ornaments, 30-43

L

Ladybug, 93-94
Leaves
    background, 68
    crocus, 34-35
    fuchsia, 102-103
    mistletoe, 41
    morning glory, 113
    sunflower, 90-91
    tulip, 58
Liner, loading, 15
Loading
    acrylic brush, 11
    liner and rake, 15
    oils, 17
Loew-Cornell Brushes, 8

M

Mail keeper, 54-63
Materials. *See* Supplies
Mistletoe, 41-42
Morning glory, 108-117

O

Oil glazing, 17, 28, 38-39, 51, 62, 72, 84, 106, 116, 124
Oils
    blending, 42
    loading brush with, 17
    setting up palette, 16
Ornaments, 30-43

P

Paints
    acrylic. *See* Acrylics
    metal, 109, 112
    oil. *See* Oils
Palette
    acrylic, 11
    oil, 16

Patterns, tracing and transferring, 10
Petals
    crocus, 35-37
    fuchsia, 103-105
    leaving space between, 48
    sunflower, 91-92
    tulip, 59
Pistils, 49, 60
Plastic wrap, into wet glaze, 48

R

Rake, loading, 15
Rice paper, for texture, 75, 78

S

Shape
    developing with values, 109
    rounded, creating illusion with floats, 104
Sideloading, 12-13
Silver leafing, 106
Slip-slapping, 68, 75, 102
Spice bin, 45-53
Sponging, 119, 122
Stained background, 87
Stamen, 49-50, 60
Stems
    crocus, 34
    morning glory, 113
    tulip, 58
Sunflower, 86-97
Supplies, 8-9
Surface, preparing, 22, 78-79, 102, 112, 122. *See also* Background

T

Techniques, 10-17
Temperature, to develop painting, 99
Tendrils, 71, 113
Texture
    with filbert rake, 55, 59, 95
    ridged, 75
Tints, adding, 72
Tray
    sunflower, 86-97
    wisteria, 64-73
Tulips, 54-63

V

Values, developing shape with, 109
Value scale, high-key, 31
Vein, center, 102

W

Walked float, 13, 31, 34-36
Washes
    color, 15
    thin, 58
Water, misting with, 11
White, warm, 16
Wildflowers, 18-29
Wisteria, 64-73

THE BEST DECORATIVE PAINTING
COMES FROM NORTH LIGHT BOOKS

The Big Book of Decorative Borders

This one-of-a-kind book is a must-have reference! With this comprehensive guide, you'll learn to create an amazing variety of borders and embellishments using the simplest of strokes. You'll find over 500 different boarder designs that you can fashion with different elements including flowers, leaves, vines, scrolls, shells, lace, ribbons, bows, children's themes and more! Also included are guidelines for measuring and marking walls and window frames to make you wall boarder painting easy!

ISBN 1-58180-335-4, paperback, 144 pages, #32303-K

Painting Gilded Florals and Fruits

Learn how to enhance your paintings with the classic elegance of decorative gold, silver, and variegated accents. Rebecca Baer illustrates detailed gilding techniques with step-by-step photos and invaluable problem-solving advice. Perfect for your home or gift-giving, there are 13 exciting projects in all, each one enhanced with lustrous leafing effects.

ISBN 1-58180-261-7, paperback, 144 pages, #32126-K

Beautiful Brushstrokes Step by Step

With Maureen McNaughton as your coach, you can learn to paint an amazing array of fabulous leaves and flowers with skill and precision. She provides start-to-finish instruction with hundreds of detailed photos. Beautiful Brushstrokes is packed with a variety of techniques, from the most basic stroke to more challenging, as well as 5 gorgeous strokework projects.

ISBN 1-58180-381-8, paperback, 128 pages #32396-K

Decorative Mini-Murals You Can Paint

Add drama to any room in your home with one of these eleven delightful mini-murals! They're perfect for when you don't have the time or experience to tackle a whole wall. You'll learn exactly which colors and brushes to use, plus tips and mini-demos on how to get that realistic "wow" effect mural painters love. Detailed templates, photos and instructions assure your success at every step

ISBN 1-58180-145-9, paperback, 144 pages, #31891-K

These and other fine North Light titles are available from your local craft retailer, bookstore, online supplier, or by calling 1-800-448-0915.